Esquire Presents

What It Feels Like

P9-DMV-966

Esquire Presents
What It Feels Like

EDITED BY A. J. JACOBS

THREE RIVERS PRESS • NEW YORK

To Walk on the Moon

To Be Gored by a Bull

To Survive an Avalanche

To Swallow Swords

To Go Over Niagara Falls in a Barrel

To Be Shot in the Head

To Win the Lottery

and Other Heights and Depths of the
Human Experience

Published by Three Rivers Press, New York, New York.
Member of the Crown Publishing Group, a division of Random House, Inc.
www.randomhouse.com

Some of the essays in this collection previously appeared in *Esquire* magazine.

THREE RIVERS PRESS and the Tugboat design are registered trademarks of Random House, Inc.

Printed in the United States of America

Design by Elizabeth Van Itallie

Library of Congress Cataloging-in-Publication Data
Esquire presents what it feels like / edited by A. J. Jacobs —1st ed.
1. Life change events—Psychological aspects.
BF637.L53E77 2003
155.9—dc21   2003004607

ISBN 0-609-80976-8

10 9 8 7 6 5 4 3 2 1

First Edition

To my wife, Julie,
who makes me feel like
I won the lottery.
(See page 54.)

ACKNOWLEDGMENTS

First, I'd like to thank David Granger, without whom there would be no "What It Feels Like," much less an *Esquire* magazine. I'd also like to thank the frighteningly talented crew he's assembled—the writers, reporters, and freelancers who actually tracked down these stories you're about to read. Among them: Mike Sager, Cal Fussman, Brendan Vaughan, Daniel Torday, Tom Colligan, Kevin McDonnell, Will Georgantas, Bryan Mealer, Gersh Kuntzman, Matt Claus, Dr. James Whitney Hall III, Jack Murnighan, Annie Silvio, Matthew Fenton, and Elizabeth Einstein. I'd also like to thank my brilliant editor, Carrie Thornton, at Three Rivers Press, my delightfully protective agent, Sloan Harris, and tenacious photo researcher Beth Johnson.

Contents

Introduction by A. J. Jacobs 12

PART 1
What It Feels Like to Battle Nature 15
What It Feels Like to Be Struck by Lightning 16
What It Feels Like to Be Buried in an Avalanche 18
What It Feels Like to Go Over Niagara Falls in a Barrel ... 20
What It Feels Like to Survive a Volcanic Eruption 23
What It Feels Like to Be Stuck in a Tornado 24
What It Feels Like to Survive a Hurricane 26
What It Feels Like to Get Frostbite 29

PART 2
What It Feels Like When Beasts Attack 33
What It Feels Like to Be Bitten by a Shark 34
What It Feels Like to Be Attacked by a Grizzly Bear 36
What It Feels Like to Be Attacked by a Swarm of
  African Killer Bees 39
What It Feels Like to Be Bitten by a Venomous Snake 41
What It Feels Like to Be Gored by a Bull 44

PART 3
What It Feels Like to Be on Top of the World 47
What It Feels Like to Walk on the Moon 48
What It Feels Like to Participate in an Orgy 52
What It Feels Like to Win the Lottery 54
What It Feels Like to Be a Mascot 57
What It Feels Like to Do Heroin 58
What It Feels Like to Win an Oscar 59
What It Feels Like to Win a Nobel Prize 62

PART 4

What It Feels Like When Diseases Strike 65

What It Feels Like to Have Amnesia 66

What It Feels Like to Have an Obsessive-
  Compulsive Disorder 68

What It Feels Like to Have the Ebola Virus 70

What It Feels Like to Have a Severe Stutter 72

What It Feels Like to Have an Epileptic Seizure 75

What It Feels Like to Have Leprosy 76

What It Feels Like to Have Narcolepsy 79

What It Feels Like to Be Albino 80

What It Feels Like to Have Tourette's Syndrome 82

What It Feels Like to Have Anorexia 84

PART 5

What It Feels Like to Battle the Unknown 87

What It Feels Like to Have Multiple Personalities
  (Dissociative Identity Disorder) 88

What It Feels Like to Undergo an Exorcism 90

What It Feels Like to Perform an Exorcism 91

PART 6

What It Feels Like to Have an Extreme Body 93

What It Feels Like to Be Really, Really Tall 94

What It Feels Like to Be Really, Really Short 96

What It Feels Like to Weigh 400 Pounds 98

What It Feels Like to Touch Fake Boobs 102

What It Feels Like to Have Fake Boobs 103

What It Feels Like to Change from a Man to a Woman ... 105

What It Feels Like to Change from a Woman to a Man ... 108

What It Feels Like to Starve 111

PART 7

What It Feels Like When People Attack 115

What It Feels Like to Get Shot in the Head 116

What It Feels Like to Be Held Hostage 118

What It Feels Like to Be a Mob Hit Man 119

What It Feels Like to Execute Someone 123

What It Feels Like to Be in Solitary Confinement 125

What It Feels Like to Swallow Swords 126

PART 8

What It Feels Like to Live and Die 129

What It Feels Like to Give Birth 130

What It Feels Like to Wake from a Coma 133

What It Feels Like to Be in a Plane Crash 134

What It Feels Like to Be 105 Years Old 136

What It Feels Like to Attempt Suicide 138

What It Feels Like to Have a Parachute Fail 140

What It Feels Like to Die 142

Introduction

Just taking a stab here, but in all likelihood, you've never walked on the moon. You've probably never won a Nobel prize, been swept up in a tornado, gone over Niagara Falls in a barrel, or been mauled by a ferocious mammal, not counting pet hamsters. And if you're like me, you've never touched fake boobs or been within shouting distance of an orgy. Even safer bet: You've never touched fake boobs after winning the Nobel prize for going over Niagara Falls in a barrel.

Not to worry. We're here to help. The profession of journalism is populated, on the whole, by a bunch of unmitigated wusses. As a professional journalist and a first-class wuss, I should know. But as voyeurs, we're fearless. There's nothing we like better than experiencing the heights and depths of the human condition—just as long as we can do it while sitting comfortably on our big butts, preferably with a nice vodka tonic within arm's reach. Which is why, for the past three years, *Esquire* magazine has collected a series of exhilarating first-person tales for our recurring feature, "What It Feels Like." The result of our exhaustive research is this disturbingly entertaining book.

Thanks to Buzz Aldrin, we can share with you what it's like to stomp your boots on the fine talcum powder that covers the moon. Thanks to a California spearfisher named Rodney Orr, we can describe the crunch of a great white shark chomping down on your skulls. Thanks to 7′6″ tall basketball star Shawn Bradley, you'll learn how it feels to peer down at the bald spots of everyone in a crowd. And thanks to an exceedingly candid man, we almost feel like we've touched the grapefruit-like orbs that are fake boobs—and without inciting the wrath of our lovely wives. Now you'll feel the same way.

The contributors featured here have been fearless—both for experiencing these things for us, and for being generous enough to tell a bunch of dorky journalists all about it. Some, like Jeff Noble, survivor of Hurricane Floyd, approached us themselves, eager to share their tales. Others we tracked down through endless phone calls and Internet searches. Still others we just stumbled on thanks to pure dumb luck (when we featured a photo spread on actress Laura Elena Harring in *Esquire*, she happened to mention that she also survived a gunshot wound). Some of these essays have appeared in *Esquire* before, but most are new to this book. Regardless, we know what it feels like to be grateful to the folks who talked to us. So sit back on your wide butt, turn the page, and read what they went through for you.

—A. J. JACOBS

Part 1
What It Feels Like
to Battle Nature

What It Feels Like to Be Struck by Lightning

[By Max Dearing, 44, sound engineer]

I have a degree in electronics, so I know about the destructive power of high-voltage energy, but this was beyond what I could have imagined. I was struck on a typical North Carolina July afternoon—little billowy clouds floating by, mostly sunny.

I was out golfing in Durham with four of my coworkers on a Friday afternoon. We were on the fifth hole when it started to sprinkle. We decided to get under a shelter and wait it out. We were standing there, just kind of harassing each other the way we always did, just talking junk. I remember the air had a sweet ozone smell to it. That's about the last thing I recall before the strike.

When the bolt hit, I was absolutely frozen, just as cold as I've ever been in my entire life, but then part of me was incredibly hot, too. I saw these red flashing lights, and I kept thinking, "It's a fire truck! A fire truck!" as if I were a little kid. Then there was the most incredible noise I'd ever heard. The sound was so loud that I honestly couldn't hear anything. Evidently, it's so loud that it blows the cilia in the ear completely flat.

I felt as if I'd been slammed between two Dumpsters. It was like every case of the flu you've ever had, at one time. My arms and my legs and my hands all felt as if they weighed 5,000 pounds. Every bit of my body was just in absolute pain. It was such a dull ache, and so sharp at the same time; it was like everything from a migraine headache to a hangover to needles being stuck in every millimeter of your body. My hair hurt, my eyelashes hurt; I could feel it when my hair moved, when the wind blew across me.

The lightning bolt had gone down along a tree next to us, taken off some branches on its way down, and then hit the overhang of the shelter, putting a huge hole in it. Then it went through Terry, one of my buddies. He was struck through the top of his head, and it came out his knee.

It killed him immediately. Then it shot up from the ground and hit the rest of us. It went up through me and left an exit wound in my head that needed eight staples. Now I have a hard time with addition and subtraction. I can handle some fairly complex math involving trigonometry and calculus, but don't ask me to add. The doctors say, "Oh, there's nothing wrong with you." But I know there is. Figuring out how to fix it, that's about like shooting mosquitoes with a shotgun.

—AS TOLD TO DANIEL TORDAY

What It Feels Like to Be Buried in an Avalanche

[By Lester Morlang, 48, contractor]

▶ My partner and I were at 12,700 feet, putting a snow shed over a gold mine in the La Plata Mountains in Colorado. My partner was Jack Ritter, and he was my mentor and my friend, may he rest in peace. It was about four o'clock in the afternoon. I was standing in the loader bucket, and Jack was handing me 12-foot-long planks. There was no warning; it was instant. All of a sudden I was curled up in a ball doing somersaults. Then it was over and I was buried. They figured out later I was under 50 feet of snow.

It was totally dark. My mouth was packed with snow. The pressure was enormous; it was hard to breathe. I literally didn't know which direction was up. I thought, "Oh my God, am I going to die like this?" And then I thought, "Oh my God, maybe I'm already dead."

Luckily I had my hands over my face. I cleared the snow out of my mouth with my fingers. And then I was screaming for Jack. You get into something like this and you absolutely lose it. It was absolute panic. I was screaming, I was bawling, I was out of my mind. The tears and snot and stuff was flowing. And then, I noticed it: All the tears was kind of running crossways across my face. I realized I was laying kind of upside down and backwards. That was a real moment of truth. Now I had a mission. I had to get out.

I moved my hands around, compacting the snow, giving myself a little more room. Then I got my upper body loose, and I started digging. I made a little game of it. I'd count to four, and then I'd reach up and grab a handful of snow. I'd pull it past my face, past my chest, down to my knees. And then with my knees I would kind of push it down to my feet and stomp it down.

I dug like that for twenty-two hours, and then I finally broke through. I jammed my hand out and saw the first little bit of light, and I was jubilant. I screamed and hollered and thanked the Lord. It was another fourteen hours till the rescuers found me. The whole experience has made me a better person. Trivial things don't bother me anymore. I can smash my finger or something, and sometimes I'll just giggle thinking how great it is to smash my finger. I guess I see a few things now that a regular person doesn't.

—AS TOLD TO MIKE SAGER

What It Feels Like TO GO OVER

[By Geoffrey Petkovich, 39, self-employed]

It takes approximately 2.3 seconds to go from the top of the falls to the bottom—which is about twenty stories. As I went over, I didn't see a thing, didn't smell a thing, didn't hear a thing. My ass was puckered up, my eyes were closed, I was holding on fuckin' tight.

Your balls go right up through your stomach and around your ears. I'm a pilot, and there are times where I'll just go up and drop it down a thousand feet. It's the same feeling.

Hitting the bottom is like getting into your car, getting it up to about 85 mph, and ramming it into the biggest tree possible. My mouth hurt most. I had a mouthpiece, and when we hit, it got driven, hard, into my upper gums. We went kerplunk into the rocks, and rolled off, and then got pushed underneath the water for another ten, fifteen seconds because of the weight of the water coming over us. That was the scary part of the ride.

The barrel took almost a year and a half to build. It started with a $1/8$-inch-thick steel shell. It's got heavy-gauge wire mesh and 8 inches of foam cork for buoyancy. It's wrapped in sheet metal and painted yellow. It weighed

3,500 pounds with me and my partner in it. Next to our heads were our oxygen tanks. In case the barrel sank, we had two hours' worth. I had two cans of beer and a pack of smokes.

Because so many people have died going over the falls, it's illegal. So we had to be sneaky. To get the barrel into the water, we put it on the back of a 5-ton steak truck we rented and catapulted it off into the river. We only had sixty seconds from the time we hit the water to the time we hit the brink of the falls. I was thinking, "Holy fuck, there ain't no turning around." I was just looking straight up at seagulls flying around and helicopters that were watching us.

Once we hit the bottom, water started coming in like crazy. That scared the living fuck out of me. But we floated down to an eddy. Our crew pulled it to the rocks. But even then, there's still danger. If you fall into the water right there, you get sucked in, the party's over for you. We made it, though.

—AS TOLD TO DANIEL TORDAY

IN A BARREL

What It Feels Like
TO SURVIVE A VOLCANIC ERUPTION

[By Thomas Mather, 22, student]

When I heard the rumble, I knew something was very very wrong. Some friends and I (including a woman I had just met a day earlier) had hiked to the top of an active volcano just outside Pacaya, Guatemala. From our vantage point, we could see small red jets of hot lava shooting out of the volcano's cone, but our guides said there was nothing to worry about; the volcano always looked like that. We could see the bursts, but not hear them—until all of a sudden, there was a slow, deep rumble that sounded like an avalanche. Then we started hearing the lava jets as they exploded hundreds of feet into the air instead of just a few. Next, a large yellow cloud—sulfurous, like rotten eggs—enveloped us. It was three in the afternoon, but the sky went black and you could feel the heat of the explosion. It was hot. Very hot. It was like you were standing right next to a raging campfire, except much, much bigger. It was so powerful, that the air pressure changed and suddenly there was a huge wind sweeping over us. Still, I didn't feel in too much danger—until I turned around and saw that our guides were running as fast as they could and shouting at us to do the same.

I started running, but a few people stayed to take pictures. One of them got hit with a bit of lava that had solidified. It cut his head right open. It was good we ran because I looked back and there was a river of oozing lava where we had been standing. Even the slowest person can outrun lava, but you can't outrun the debris that comes raining down on you. When we had gotten down to the base camp and were on our bus three miles away, lava rocks continued to pelt the tin roof of the bus. But we were safe. And that woman I had just met? We ended up dating and getting married. It was probably because we always had something exciting to talk about after that volcano.

—AS TOLD TO GERSH KUNTZMAN

What It Feels Like to Be Stuck in a Tornado

[By John L. Neidigh, 43, Web designer/tree farmer]

As the old joke goes, in Mississippi, divorces and tornadoes have one thing in common. Somebody's gonna lose a trailer. Little did I know that when my wife announced that she hated Mississippi that spring day, I would experience both by year's end. On December 9, 1999, I arrived home from work, flipped on the tube, and the weatherman broke into the high school football report.

I had only enough time to lie down on the living room floor and cover my head with my arms. I remember saying to myself, "Okay, you're dead. But at least you're going to live long enough to experience what it's like inside a tornado." The feel of a twister approaching is exactly the feel of a freight train approaching—that low, ever-louder howl and the shuddering ground. First, a sheet of rain sprayed against the entire side of the trailer like machine-gun fire. I could hear trees snapping and debris shooting through the trailer: swoosh, thunk, thunk—in one side and out the other.

The plastic skirting blew off, the aluminum siding and roof metal began ripping off, and the whole length of the trailer began moving up and down in a wave-like fashion. The hurricane straps that bolted my trailer to the ground began vibrating in an eerie, low frequency until they all snapped: pop, pop, pop, pop.

Just as I felt the entire trailer lift off the ground and begin to rotate, I blacked out. I woke up twenty minutes later facedown outside the house, on top of a rock the size of a pumpkin. The evening was completely quiet: There was no wind, no cars, no insect noises. Most of the contents of the mobile home were scattered across the cotton fields or lodged in the branches of the trees on the far side of the farm. The mobile-home frame was bent like a horseshoe around the branches of an oak tree.

I had gone through the trailer wall, been thrown 30 feet up into the tree, and then dropped to the ground. I had a concussion, collapsed lung, some cracked ribs, my head was huge, and my face was completely black and blue (I was told I looked like a raccoon). My spine was compressed in a couple places, my lower left leg was shattered (most of the muscles were ripped off my shin and calf), my pelvis was crushed, and I was spread open like a pig ready for the chitlins pot. The injuries I sustained should have killed anyone, not to mention someone who deals with "manual metabolism" 24/7 (type 1 diabetes since age seven). The surgeons, bless their hearts, returned my chitlins to their rightful pot, pinned, strapped, screwed, and sewed me back together.

What It Feels Like

TO SURVIVE A HURRICANE

[By Jeff Noble, 42, professional estate manager]

Circumstance had forced my hand; I had relocated to a crappy little town in eastern North Carolina known as Rocky Mount. I accepted a position as a personal chef / estate manager, aka professional ass wiper.

When I awoke the morning of September 17, 1999, at 6:00 A.M., I knew even before I got out of bed that something was wrong. As soon as I put my feet on the floor, I was up to my ankles in filthy water. I ran to the front of the house and looked out to see my very serious predicament. The muddy water had already covered my car and was moving very fast to the north. After trying the phone and then the cell phone, neither of which worked, I knew this was very real and really serious. I started to panic. I could taste the hot, coppery adrenaline in my mouth.

I gathered together the most important things, my dad's will, my personal papers, some clean clothes in a garbage bag, and most crucially, my .45 automatic and two boxes of shells. I got a length of rope and opened my front door. *Hell with the lid off* is the best description I could give to what was happening outside. Water rushed into my house as I stepped out on the porch. I threw my briefcase and garbage bag onto the roof. Then I tied the rope around my waist and around one of the porch supports. The wind was howling with an intensity I have never heard before. Large trees were snapping like twigs. Transformers popped and utility poles fell like matchsticks. I forced the fear back down inside and waited. When there was a lull in the wind, I fired three shots in the air, three being the international distress signal. I screamed at the top of my lungs, and scared the shit out of myself. Never knew I could scream that loud. An hour, maybe two, had passed and I realized that water had risen to my thighs on the porch. I had spent over half my ammo, I was soaking wet and starting to get cold. Things proceeded to get worse. A huge oak tree bashed into the porch, knocking down the support post that I was tied to. I was slammed up against the front of the house.

I frantically tried to pull at the knot I had tied as the support post sank. I was pulled under into the water. I shoved my gun into my pants as I looked up and could make out the gray sky above the water. Raindrops smashed into the water as debris rushed past. My breath was running out as I pulled at the slippery knot. How the fuck could this be happening? One day I'm making great money and living large and the next I'm fighting for my life under water. I was wasting oxygen, so I got as calm as I could, reached into my pocket for my keys. At the end of my key chain was a tiny knife. I pulled it up and managed to get the knife blade out. I began sawing through the thick rope, hoping I wouldn't drop the knife. I was running out of oxygen fast. I was doing everything by feel and I could feel I was halfway through the rope. Not good enough. I felt my consciousness leaving me. I hacked and sawed like a madman possessed. What felt like hours was only minutes. The last strands were near and I had to get a breath or die trying. Finally, the rope was cut through. Now I had to get up to the surface without being swept away by the current.

I pulled my way along the rope until I felt the tree wedged against the house. The root end was jutting out of water only a few feet away. I grabbed and pulled my way along the tree until I felt a raging wind across my face. It was as if I had stuck my head out the window of a 747. I collapsed on the high end of the tree, my lungs burning as they filled with air. After several minutes I retrieved my gun and resumed firing. Even soaked with water and mud, it did what it was designed to do, make a lot of noise. Hypothermia was slowly setting in to my wet body. Four and a half hours after going onto my porch, some passersby in a boat heard my gunshots. They rescued me. They restored my core temperature and saved my life as I had earlier saved my own. This is my story about Hurricane Floyd. Nearly drowning was a horrible experience. Being given a second chance at life was a thrill I couldn't and still can't describe. Making the most out of that chance is what I do now.

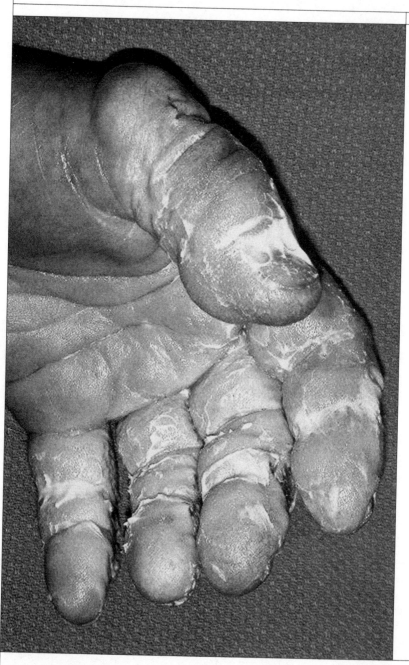

What It Feels Like
TO GET FROSTBITE

[By Sir Ranulph Fiennes, 59, explorer]

It was a full moon that night, and the temperature was −45 degrees Fahrenheit. In the moonlight, the arctic landscape resembles a fairyland. There are ice blocks of every shape and size, and they can look like elephants or skyscrapers or demons, and the snow is just the most lovely color.

I was a week into attempting the first solo, unsupported trek to the North Pole from Canada. Before leaving, I had worked it out that the trip would take eighty days and I would need about 500 pounds of kit and food. Being fifty-five years old and pretty geriatric, I had to divide it between two sledges, which meant that for every mile I moved, I had to ski three, leapfrogging the sledges. Now, −45 degrees is cold, but if there's no wind, it's really lovely. Unfortunately there was a wind of 5 knots, and even that cuts any exposed flesh like a knife.

If you were foolish enough to put a ball of snow in your mouth, it would burn the flesh off your tongue.

I had come upon a 30-foot-high wall of ice that night. I managed to get to the top of the wall when one of the sledges started sliding over the other side. I grabbed it and held on, but it weighed 300 pounds and dragged me over the edge. The sledge was badly damaged, so I had to backtrack many miles to Ward Hunt Island, where I knew there was an abandoned hut; I had built it on an expedition twenty years earlier.

I repaired the sledge and set out a second time. All was going well when I came to an area of broken ice with a lot of black sea, plenty of movement. The ice was making a lot of noise—like Tchaikovsky, which is bad for the imagination. I was towing the first sledge when it slipped sideways down a ridge and slid about 10 feet into the sea. I clattered down the ridge, and my foot and ski went into the water. I needed to pull the sledge out, simple as that. It had the radio, the beacon, and seventy days' worth of food. But somewhere underneath the ice blocks, the rope was snagged.

I couldn't get it out without lying on my stomach and putting my hand in. You can't wear waterproof gloves because they don't sweat, so I took the mitts off my left hand and fiddled around under the water, and luckily I unsnagged it. The water wasn't all that cold—probably about 30 degrees Fahrenheit. But when I got my arm out of the water, it started getting cold very quickly. My fingers—which were clenched around the rope with 300 pounds at the other end—felt like dead wood. They weren't bendable.

My feet were slipping, and I was standing on an ice block that was sinking. So it was a sticky situation. It was about five minutes of extreme work to drag the sledge back to the top. When I got there, my first thought was to get blood back down into my fingers. You do this with a simple windmill motion, which uses centrifugal force to make the blood go down. It was the first time in my life that the blood didn't go back down. My fingers had gone past the point of no return. Then I was getting whole-body shivers, which I've seen in other people over the years. I knew I didn't have very long to do two things—one, to get the tent up, and two, to start the gasoline stove to warm up my hand. Both of these things you can easily do with two hands, but with one hand that's got no feeling and the other getting numb, you need to be very quick.

I put up the tent partially. I couldn't handle the matches, but I had a lighter. I held the stove-control knob in my mouth and lit it with my good hand. After warming my hand, I skied eight hours back to the hut on Ward Hunt Island. I was in a bad way. I got the beacon going and got in touch with the bush pilots down in Resolute Bay. They diverted a ski plane, and I found old tins and rags in the hut, poured some of the cooking fuel on them, and lit them near a flat bit of sea ice. The pilot made an incredible landing, and I eventually ended up in Ottawa General Hospital.

I stayed in an oxygen chamber for a total of sixty hours. Then I went back to the U.K., where a British navy expert explained that frostbite amputation should wait until at least five months after the accident because the semidamaged areas take that long to get back to the point where they can be pulled as flaps over the newly cut areas.

The dead ends of my fingers were very black, and every time I touched one of them against something, it was agonizing. Eventually I thought, "Well, why don't I get rid of them?" So I used a Black & Decker vise and a saw in the toolshed. It wasn't painful, but going through the bones was quite difficult. It felt better afterward, since I was much less likely to hit things with my fingers. The surgeon would later be upset that I did that.

More than half of my thumb had to be cut off, and about one third of the other four fingers went. Now I can do everything except button my right-hand sleeve. I just have a problem with the cold. My hand doesn't like the cold. But that will improve.

—AS TOLD TO DANIEL TORDAY

Sir Ranulph Fiennes has been listed in the Guinness Book of Records *as "The World's Greatest Living Explorer." His team was the first to circumnavigate the globe on its polar axis, and he was the first (with Dr. Mike Stroud) to make an unsupported trek across the Antarctic Continent. He is also a cousin of actors Ralph and Joseph Fiennes.*

Part 2
What It Feels Like
When Beasts Attack

What It Feels Like to Be Bitten by a Shark

[By Rodney Orr, 62, electrician]

▶ I was on my paddleboard in the Pacific near Santa Rosa, California. I was getting ready to dive off the side and go spearfishing when the lights went out. I heard this big, loud noise like a garage door slamming, and it was completely dark. Then all of a sudden I could see these big white things out of my left eye. At first I thought it was busted fiberglass. I thought maybe a boat ran over me and stuffed my head through my board. But as soon as I touched the white things, I realized that those were teeth.

He had a hold of my head. I was at a right angle to its mouth, hanging out the side. The front teeth were buried in through my cheekbones and my nose. It was quick and sharp. The teeth were like razors. When he clamped on to me, it was a God-awful crunch. I heard the crunching and the teeth plow through the bone, but it didn't hurt. Something in the brain clicks so you don't feel it till later.

He didn't take me down—he took me out of the water. When I saw the water, it was like 3 feet below, but I could see we were moving fast. I tried to pull my head out. I reached up on the shark and it was flat, like the side of a Buick, and it had a kind of sandpapery feel. And then I just started pounding on it. I went berserk. I shredded my gloves on his teeth. I was just striking at him blind. I don't know if that's what made him let loose of me. If he would've finished the bite, I would've had no brain.

When he let go, he went underneath me, and I saw part of

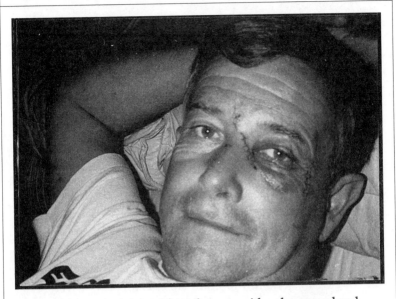

his head. He was a great white; he was wider than my shoulders. He had a hold of me for eight to twelve seconds. We probably traveled about 60 to 70 feet. I swam back to my board. I was bleeding like hell, just blood pouring out of my nose, out of my face. The board was upside down, so I grabbed the side of the board and I flipped it over and it flopped upright. I couldn't feel nothing from the top of my head to the butt on the right side. I had a $2\frac{1}{4}$-inch hole in the back of my neck. I was choking and spitting out all this blood that was running down the back of my throat. And I said, "I gotta get to shore. Now." They took me away in a helicopter and I got to Santa Rosa hospital. I had like thirty-five or forty stitches in the front and probably twenty-five or thirty in the back. They had no mirrors at the hospital. The only glimpse I caught was a reflection on the helicopter window. I looked like hamburger. Now, I've got one bad scar near the corner of my eye and across my nose, but hell, they've faded down and fit in the wrinkles.

—AS TOLD TO MATT CLAUS

What It Feels Like to Be Attacked by a Grizzly Bear

[By Steve Chamberlain, 51, orthopedic surgeon]

The sun is setting, and my partner, Dave Wood, and I are bow hunting for elk in the Madison Mountains of Montana. We're lying down, exhausted after a long day of hiking, hunting, and not seeing any elk. Dave makes one loud big-bull bugle call. Suddenly footfalls are crashing explosively downhill at us faster than hell. I think, "A bull elk is charging!" But instead three grizzly bears loom up with dirt and rocks flinging back from their feet—a huge sow and two big yearlings!

The bears leap over Dave and—so fast I can't jerk my right hand from my arrow to my pistol—the sow is on me biting my left leg. Snap goes the bone. I can't free my gun. Now she's chewing my calf, yanking me with unbelievable force, and she's gashing up my thigh when she throws me around like a toy. It's a deadly tug-of-war. I know I'm supposed to play dead, but I can't do it, I've gotta fight, and I'm screaming, "She's mauling me—get her off!" I strike her in the face.

She grabs my left arm, tearing the muscles and tendons, and tosses me in the air. Then she attacks my head as I'm airborne. All I can see is her open mouth, her muzzle fringed with silver hair. I twist away my face just in time and headbutt her, but her teeth are gashing my scalp and ear. I can hear her fangs grinding on my skull, and I think: "I'm losing. This is it. The next bite will kill me."

But just then, she turns away. I get my pistol out but crumple to the ground as my broken leg collapses. Dave has come after her with pepper spray. Now I can see him sprawled on the ground near my feet, and he's helpless after spray blew back into his face. He's blinded, tears streaming from his eyes. I'm bleeding like a stuck pig, blood pouring into my ear and down my neck. I take stock of my body parts—what's still attached, what works? Pain suddenly over-whelms me totally and I hear myself screaming . . . And I'm waiting for the inevitable return of the bears.

I manage a few steps despite my left foot flopping from broken bone and crushed muscles. But I am really weak, and any movement of the ankle was killing, and spasms of pain shoot to my waist between steps. I finally get some control of the agony, realizing I have to ignore the pain to survive. So despite my mangled left arm and leg draining blood, I manage to stumble after Dave on the rough ground two miles in full dark to an old skid trail.

Dave covered me with his coat and ran three miles for our car. Lying there, cold and shaking from shock, I knew I'd left a blood trail, and sounds of large animals pass by—they could be bear or cougar. Staring at bright stars overhead, I'm thinking: "I've got no fight left. I'm powerless, impotent to control my fate. It's out of my hands."

Dave returns, bundles me into the car, and speeds over ninety miles to the hospital in Bozeman, where an orthopedic surgeon operates on me for more than three hours.

I feel no grudge against the grizzly. She heard the bugle, thought I was an elk, and being the ultimate predator, came to dinner. I'm incredibly lucky. If she'd used her claws, she'd easily have disemboweled me. The ferocious mauling took *five seconds!* And Dave saved my life. Would I have had the courage to charge that grizzly, the world's biggest carnivore, armed only with a tiny spray can, to save his life? What did I learn? Always be ready and wary. Know your and your partner's outdoor skills. Don't bugle unless you're prepared to take immediate action. And, in grizzly country, always carry pepper spray, and you might carry a gun. I have magnified respect for the grizzly's awesome speed, power, and intelligence.

—AS TOLD TO DR. JAMES WHITNEY HALL III

What It Feels Like

TO BE ATTACKED BY A SWARM OF AFRICAN KILLER BEES

[By Michael Finkel, 34, writer and chicken farmer]

Buzz.

Buzz-buzz.

Buzz-buzz-buzz-buzz-buzz.[1]

Buzzzzzzzzz.

Buzzzzzzzzzzzzzzzzzzzzzzzzzzzzzzzz.

Buzzzzzzzzzzzzzzzzzzzzzzzzzzzzzzzzzzzzzzzzzzzzzzzzzzzzzzzzzzzzzzzz
zzzzzzzzzzzzzz.

Buzzzzzzzzzzzzzzzzzzzzzzzzzzzzzzzzzzzzzzzzzzzzzzzzzzzzzzzzzzzzzzzz
zzzzzzzzzzzzzzzzzzzzzzzzzzzzzzzzzzzzzzzzzzzzzzzzzzzzzzzzzzzzzzzzzz
zzzzzzzzzzzzzzzzzzzzzzzzzzzzzzzzzzzzzzzzzzzzzzzzzzzzzzzzzzzzzzzeee
eeeeeeeeeeeeeeeeeeeeeeeeeeeeeeeeeeeeeeeeeeeeeeeeeeeeeeeeeeeeeeeee
eeeeeeeeeeeeeeeeeeeeeeeeeeeeeeeeeeeeeeeeeeeeeeeeeeeeeeeeeeeeeeeee
eeeeeeeeeeeeeeeeeeeeeeeeeeeeeeee.[2]

Ouch.

Ouch!

Ouch-ouch-ouch.

Ouch-ouch-ouch-ouch-ouch-ouch-ouch-ouch-ouch-ouch-ouch-
ouch-ouch.[3]

Fuckin' ouch!

Fuck-o-fuck-o-fuck-o-fuck-o-fuck.[4]

Fuck!

Fuckfuckfuckfuckfuck fuckfuckfuckfuckfuckfuck fuckfuckfuckfuckfuckfuck fuckfuckfuckfuckfuckfuck

fuckfuckfuckfuckfuckfuck fuckfuckfuckfuckfuckfuck fuckfuck.

"Run, Mike! Run, run, run!"[5]

Tramp-tramp-tramp-tramp-tramp-tramp-tramp-tramp-tramp-
tramp-tramp-tramp-tramp.

Buzzzzzzzz.

Tramptramptramptramptramptramptramptramptramptramptramp
tramptramptramptramptramp
tramptramptramptramptramptramptramptramptramptramptramp.[6]

Oh . . . oh . . . oh . . . oh . . . oh . . . oh . . .

Oh, thank fuckin' God.[7]

1. They emerged from a nest hidden beneath a rock, near where I was hiking in central Africa. They came at me like fighter jets.

2. At a certain critical mass, the buzz stopped being a buzz. The sound became like a dentist's drill—a piercing, shrieking whine.

3. The sting is sharp and quick and weirdly extractive. It feels less like something jabbing into you than like a small piece of you being yanked out. The immediate sensation is of heat—a flash of fire at the stinger's point of impact—then pain, the type of dizzy, nauseous pain that throbs at your fingertips.

4. My face was a mask of bees; I could not see. I clawed at the insects, but my clawing only further enraged them. My brain locked, a grand mal seizure of primal fear.

5. My friend Randy was shouting. It's an obvious thing to do, running, but in my frenzy I hadn't thought of it.

6. I ran over boulders and bushes and termite mounds. After a minute or so, the swarm released me.

7. If I'd been even mildly allergic, the bees would have lived up to their name. My head was pincushioned with stingers, two dozen of them, and had already inflamed to watermelonesque proportions. It took two weeks before the swelling subsided. I'm still waiting for the memories to do the same.

What It Feels Like to Be Bitten by a Venomous Snake

[By "Gator" John Kenyon, 37, reptile specialist/entertainer]

I guess it was my own damn fault. I had been feeding snakes in the back and didn't wash off my arm properly. Next thing, I'm on stage doing a snake show, like I do three times a day at Billie Swamp Safari on the Big Cypress Seminole Indian reservation. I had just pulled a northern copperhead out of a box with the snake hook to show her to the crowd. I remember this distinctly: I had just told them that the reason that so many people are bitten by northern copperheads is not because the snake is aggressive, but because it's so common throughout the entire eastern half of the United States. Just as I said that, I took my eyes off her for just a second. She must have smelled the mice and rats on me because she sunk her fangs into my right forearm, just below the elbow. It didn't hurt; it was just a pinch or like someone had grabbed my skin with a pair of pliers and pulled lightly.

My adrenaline was pumping because I was on stage, so I didn't react immediately. In fact, I remember saying, "Look how this snake is biting me." I even looked at the crowd and saw that everyone's expressions were normal. There was no alarm because most people think snakes are milked before a show. Well, they're not.

Now, drop per drop, this snake's venom has extremely low potency. But she had her fangs in me for a full five seconds. And

then I felt the burning of the venom under my skin. This venom is a hemotoxin, meaning it breaks down muscle tissue. So I just pushed my fingers against my biceps to block the flow and called for backup. I didn't even get through the sentence "Gator John to gift shop: I've just been bitten by a venomous snake" before there were two guys on me. I was really brave in front of the crowd, but when they got me out the door, my body got cold and clammy all over. And my brain was going through all the permutations: "Am I going to lose my entire arm?" "Is this going to spread to my chest cavity and kill my heart?" "Am I going to be able to hold my kids again?" I was in tears just from all the emotions.

Before I knew it, I was in a helicopter heading for the hospital, where I was met by the Miami Dade snake experts, who made sure the hospital didn't kill me. At this point, my right forearm looked like Popeye's. The pain didn't happen right away. When it started to swell is when I felt the pain. It wasn't throbbing, exactly, but there was a burning sensation. The swelling finally got up to my lymph nodes under my armpit, but the intense part of the pain went up to my elbow. The doctors originally wanted to raise my arm so the swelling would go down, but that would've sent the venom straight to my heart. And they were originally going to give me the wrong anti-venom because they thought I—a snake expert!—had misidentified the one that bit me. It's a good thing I wasn't unconscious! When the blood test came back, it showed that there was three times more venom in this bite than a normal bite. So they pumped ten vials of anti-toxin into me, which is a lot considering most people get a half-vial. I recovered quickly and to this day, the only lasting reminder of the bite is the slight brown discoloration under my skin from the venom. Oh, and also my son, who used to pick up snakes like other kids pick up toys, no longer picks one up without first asking me what kind it is.

—AS TOLD TO GERSH KUNTZMAN

What It Feels Like to Be Gored by a Bull

[By George Sutton, 58, cattle station manager]

▶ It was my first day on the job as station manager at Balbarini in the Northern Territory of Australia and I was getting the lay of the land. I was going along a boundary fence and noticed a bull sitting under a tree. I went to check on him, but he got up and I just knew the bastard was going to come at me.

I started moving back, but he charged me, so I just started running. But he got me before I could get back to the truck. The bloody Devil was playing Ping-Pong with me between his two horns.

At one point, I was just hanging off one of his horns. It felt like someone cut me in half with a cane knife. You could hear the ripping sound, like I was being unzipped. There was blood everywhere. My ribs were up near my eyes and I just thought I was a goner. I finally got him off me by jabbing him in the eyes. My stomach was pierced in two places and my lower abdomen was exposed. My kidney was just hanging out there. So I took my shirt and wrapped it around me—more to keep my guts inside than to stop the bleeding—and then had to drive 4 kilometers back to the Balbarini Homestead.

They wrapped me in a beach towel and a belt and laid me in the back of a Toyota truck to take me to the airstrip at Borroloola. I rode 110 kilometers with my legs hanging out the back of the truck on a road that was like Hell itself. In Borroloola, they lined up six Toyotas on the field so a plane could land and take me to Darwin. They operated on me for five hours, and through it all, I never got any dope. I'd lost two thirds of my blood and it took 480 stitches to close me up. I was in the hospital for two months. When I came out, I was 175 pounds. I'm usually 235. I looked terrible. Now I have scars that start from the top of my rib cage and go all around to my backbone and from my belly button to my armpit. And under my right breast, I have a hole you could hold a hamburger in. There's supposed to be muscle there, but it's just bone. It's probably taken ten years off my life, but I just keep working. The other day, I drove 360 cows up to a dam 15 kilometers from here. You just can't throw in the towel.

—AS TOLD TO GERSH KUNTZMAN

Part 3

What It Feels Like to Be on Top of the World

What It Feels Like to Walk on the Moon

[By Buzz Aldrin, 73, astronaut]

The surface of the moon was like fine talcum powder. It was very loose at the top. As you begin to get deeper, a half inch or so, it becomes much more compact, almost as if it's cemented together, though it isn't. It just seems that way because there are no air molecules between the molecules of dust.

When you put your foot down in the powder, the boot-print preserved itself exquisitely. When I would take a step, a little semicircle of dust would spray out before me. It was odd, because the dust didn't behave at all the way it behaves here on Earth. On Earth, you're sometimes dealing with puffy dust, sometimes with sand. On the moon, what you're dealing with is this powdery dust traveling through no air at all, so the dust is kicked up, and then it all falls at the same time in a perfect semicircle.

I'm trying the best I can to put it into words, but being on the moon is just different—different from anything you've ever seen. To use the word *alien* would mislead people. *Surreal* is probably as good a word as I have. When I looked out the window of the lunar lander as we touched down, the sun was out, the sky was velvety black, the engine was shut down, and everything was silent. That was surreal.

When you're on the moon, there's very little audio around you, only the sounds of your suit—the hum of pumps circulating fluid. But you don't hear any amplified breathing inside your mask; that's a Hollywood contrivance. The name of the game on the moon is stay cool and don't exert too much so you're never out of breath.

If you remember the television images we sent back, you know that I was attempting to demonstrate different walking motions, going back and forth in front of the camera. I tried what you might call a kangaroo hop, and then I demonstrated how you needed a few steps to change direction because of the inertia that you have up there. I found that the best way to move around at a fairly good clip was not by using a jogging motion—one foot, then the other—but rather by moving more the way a horse gallops: one-two, one-two, two steps in

rapid succession, followed by a lope, followed by two more rapid steps.

And then there's the picture where I'm standing next to the flag. If you notice, I'm leaning forward a good bit because of the center of gravity of the backpack I'm wearing. On the moon, it's sometimes hard to tell when you might be on the verge of losing your balance. As you lean a little bit to one side or the other, you come in danger of falling. But it's easy to right yourself by pushing down on the surface with your feet. The lunar surface is so easy, so natural, so readily adapted to by any human being. The low gravity makes it very convenient to get around. It's really a very nice environment.

While we were on the moon, there wasn't time to savor the moment. It seemed as though what we were doing was so significant that to pause for a moment and reflect metaphysically was really contrary to our mission. We weren't trained to smell the roses. We weren't hired to utter philosophical truisms on the spur of the moment. We had a job to do.

I do remember that one realization wafted through my mind when I was up there. I noted that here were two guys farther away from anything than two guys had ever been before. That's what I thought about. And yet, at the same time, I was very conscious that everything was being closely scrutinized a quarter of a million miles away.

Everything and anything we did would be recorded, remembered, studied for ages. It felt a little like being the young kid in the third or fourth grade who is all of a sudden asked to go up on stage in front of the whole school and recite the Gettysburg Address. And as he tries to remember the words, he's got gun-barrel vision. He's not seeing what's going on around him; he's focused on that particular task, conscious only of his performance. It was like that but even more so. The eyes of the world were on us, and if we made a mistake, we would regret it for quite a while.

I guess, if I look back on things, there was one little moment of levity, a bit of unusual extemporaneousness. When the countdown came to lift off from the moon, when it got to twenty seconds, Houston said, "Tranquility Base, you're cleared for liftoff." And I said in response: "Roger, we're number one on the runway." Now, comedy is the absurd put into a natural position. There was no runway up there. And there certainly wasn't anyone else waiting in line to lift off. I was conscious of that, of being first.

—AS TOLD TO MIKE SAGER

What It Feels Like

TO PARTICIPATE IN AN ORGY

[Anonymous]

At their best, orgies are like sex with a trained octopus: many limbs, many tongues, hands grabbing and pulling, legs being opened, your mouth filled, too much for the brain to process, too much for the libido that got you into it. At their worst, orgies are like Third World tourist sites on a hot day: too many hands reaching for you, each wanting something you could provide but aren't really in the mood to—a hungry crowd you resent for its hunger.

Orgies, like any anonymous sex, let you see just how ugly unshielded desire can be. Unless the host or hostess is extremely capable and assembles a genetically engineered cast, orgies tend not to be populated quite with whom you'd hope. The women—yes, they're available, but most benefit from dim light and the de rigueur excess of makeup. And the men—every orgy seems to have way too many men, with all their dicks, guts, and body hair sticking out, pawing sad little clappers in desperate attempts to get them up. Freud might think we're all a little gay, but we certainly aren't gay enough to appreciate so much of the same.

And yet, despite this, the orgy can provide experiences you won't find elsewhere: the odd thrill of hearing grunty rutting close by; the women, one and then another and another; the incomparable sensation of entering a woman who's already being entered and feeling another man through the not-so-thick membrane; the frenzy of making a mess of your sexual categories. And all the while, the thought that keeps going through your mind (and through the cab ride home, and into breakfast the next day): "I'm at an orgy! I'm at an orgy!"

—AS TOLD TO JACK MURNIGHAN

What It Feels Like to Win the Lottery

[By Ed Brown, 50, mayor of Washington, Iowa]

When you play the lottery a lot, you check the numbers in the paper every week. Well, on Christmas Eve morning, 1992, I checked the numbers, but this time, all six matched. I'd won $5 million. I checked it again and then I stood up and turned around and sat back down. I didn't know what to do. It's like reading your own obituary. It's like experiencing every emotion at once.

It was six in the morning and my wife and kids were still in bed, but I didn't even wake them up. I just got ready and went to the nursing home where I worked as director of maintenance. I found that I couldn't concentrate on anything, so I only did the easy things, like changing lightbulbs. Anything complicated, I let my helper do. I didn't want to be doing anything that required a lot of thinking, like replacing faucets. I went home for lunch and one of my sons said, "Dad, the radio says that someone from Washington won the Powerball." I just said, "Well, it wasn't me." But when they left, I told my wife, "It was me." And she just turned pale. We just sat and talked for a while about what we should do next. I still felt off. You get this feeling of dread, like something is going to go wrong.

This was a Thursday and the lottery office in Des Moines wouldn't open until Monday, so we rented a safe-deposit box for the weekend and put the ticket there. Then I went to the liquor store to get a case of champagne for my mother's Christmas party. Usually, I just bring a casserole. On Monday, we drove to Des Moines, talking all the way in the car about how we'd spend the money. My sons wanted new cars. I told them, "I won the lottery, not you." (I ended up buying them used cars.)

When I got there, I still had that feeling that the woman would run the ticket through the machine and say, "Oh, my goodness, there's been a horrible mistake." But she ran it through and just said, "Congratulations, Mr. Brown." I filled out paperwork and two weeks later, I got my first check: $175,000 after taxes. At the time, my family income was $40,000 a year.

My wife and I actually kept working for a year—she worked in a calendar factory—because we just weren't ready to be retired. Finally, I quit and the next year, I ran for mayor and won. The mayor's salary is $6,399 a year, but I don't take it; I donate it to a senior citizens' program. I've always been a simple guy, so I don't think winning has changed me. I mean, after I won the lottery, I went out and bought a fancy pair of leather gloves. And then they got torn and I felt really bad about the wasted money and all. And I thought, "I don't need to get upset over a pair of gloves." So now I'm back to buying the $1.99 gloves and not worrying. I guess I liked who I was before I won the lottery and I decided not to change.

—AS TOLD TO GERSH KUNTZMAN

What It Feels Like
TO BE A MASCOT

[By Ted Giannoloulas, 49, the San Diego Chicken]

The suit goes on in about ten minutes. It consists of nine different pieces—a furry jumpsuit with a foam tail and head, a couple of feet, white gloves, a vest, and a set of leotards. It weighs about 7 pounds, and as costumes go, that's very light. I can see a little bit out of the beak.

There is no air conditioning, no ice packs. On average it's about 110 degrees in there, and I build up a really heavy sweat. It's like a rainforest in there. But I'm used to it, because I'm from Canada— I used to be a hockey goalie. Put on 40 pounds of goalie gear and you'll be conditioned to sweating a lot. Because the suit's made of foam, it airs out, so it doesn't smell bad at all. And I am meticulous about that, because I have a very close proximity to the fans, and I can't be gamy.

I hire a staff to look after the suit. I travel around the country in a tour bus. For a recent tour, I used the rock band Creed's bus.

In twenty-nine years, I haven't missed a single game to injury or illness. The greatest moment of my life was my "Grand Hatching" in June of 1979. I sold out the Murph. I was brought in in a 10-foot Styrofoam egg atop an armored truck, escorted on the field by California Highway Patrol; all the ballplayers came out and took me off of the roof and I hatched out of the egg. Ten-minute standing ovation, and I'll tell you, I know how Lou Gehrig felt at that moment. I made $40,085. That night I was the highest-paid athlete in the world.

I used to do this little sketch where I would hijack a basket of peanuts from one of the vendors and hand them out to the audience. Ray Kroc thought that was hysterical. He would personally send the ushers down to remind me, "Please hijack the peanuts." Kroc was one of the finest people I've ever met. He said to me, "We're losing 7–2 here, and my customers are laughing. Anything you want, you come and see me personally."

—AS TOLD TO DANIEL TORDAY

What it Feels Like TO DO HEROIN

[By David "Wilson," 41, former addict]

You do heroin and bang: You get instant, total relief from whatever ails you. Everything just falls away. Physical pain, psychic pain, everything. The scales fall off your eyes and your heart. Your stiff neck goes away. You don't care anymore that your girlfriend just dumped you. Everything is suddenly perfect; all is right with the world—sudden, definite, bearable lightness of being. Inhibitions are lifted. If you're a shy person, you'll be able to talk. If you're meditative, you can enjoy it alone, just nodding off. And you know, there's a thing about the nod. The deal with the nod is you don't want to waste your high by falling asleep. So you keep yourself awake, just on the edge, dancing heroically on the edge. You're really aware of yourself as meat, but in a strangely transcendent way. You're there but you're not. "Drifting," like Hendrix said, "on a sea of forgotten teardrops."

When you're addicted to heroin, your entire existence becomes ordered around these north and south poles of want and wellness, and it's odd to realize— beyond dope sick and just raw need—how it organizes you down to your cellular level. After a while you stop wanting to go out. The addict in isolation is a perfectly self-contained unit. Everybody looks at you with reproach, but you don't care about anybody else if you're high. Because you are married to dope. It's more than half your life. It is your life. All you want is to be high. And if you're sick, all you want is to get right. It all comes down to one thing: The first time you did heroin you felt better than you'd ever felt in your entire life.

—AS TOLD TO
MIKE SAGER

What It Feels Like to Win an Oscar

[By Steve Gaghan, 38, screenwriter of Traffic]

I worked the day of the Academy Awards. I worked and tried to pretend it was a normal day and I succeeded in this fiction for a long while, right through the *hair and makeup person* in our bathroom doing my fiancée's hair and makeup, through the limousine arriving, through the attempt to scribble on a 3x5 card a list of people to thank while sitting in a traffic jam outside the Dorothy Chandler Pavilion, through getting elbowed out of the way by Roger Ebert as he lunged for a more interesting person to interview, through the canyon of fans screaming names, even my own, into our seats where I was able to stare at Sting's neck from about 18 inches away while famous people milled around commenting on each other's appearances.

The excitement and strangeness and self-importance of awards shows can really do a number on your head. It's possible to start to believe it's important to have been nominated and even more important to win. It's possible to become brainwashed by the lights and red carpets and jewels into wanting to win so badly that you must counteract this thought by telling yourself it doesn't really matter, that it's great just to have been considered, and the tension between these two modes of thinking seems to steadily remove the oxygen from the theater. They announced that after a commercial we'd be right back with Tom Hanks and the category of Best Adapted Screenplay. My fiancée, Michael, squeezed my hand. I'm thinking I've heard them say that *we'll be right back* phrase before, but I was in my living room looking at the television. Michael squeezed my hand again, harder. I turned. She said, "Let's meditate." I stared at her. I must have looked like a cow as the conveyor belt lifts its feet off the ground. "Just close your eyes and breathe," she said.

I opened my eyes and was staring up into a 60-foot-high image of what looked like Dr. Strangelove. I thought, "Oh, I love that movie." A man in a wheelchair with a blanket on his legs surrounded by blooming flowers via satellite feed from . . . Sri Lanka? Where? A recorded announcement was talking about *2001: A Space Odyssey*. What? It's Arthur C. Clarke. Who? He has an envelope. He's announcing something about "the nominees are . . ." I hear my own name. I realize again that I'm at the Academy Awards. Arthur C. Clarke is presenting via satellite from Colombo, Sri Lanka. Of course. Michael squeezes my hand. She said, "Be present and always remember this moment."

Arthur C. Clarke said my name for the first and probably last time. I turned toward Michael. I told her I loved her. She had "tears in her eyes." I'm so present, I think, that even now, I'm thinking in quotes. I start down the aisle. I hug Steven Soderbergh and Ed Zwick and Ed's wife, Liberty. I think, "Hey, this is going to be all right. I feel okay. I'm here. I'm calm. I can do this." I turn the corner and look up into the faces of thousands of people in black tie staring at me, except for Michael Douglas and Catherine Zeta-Jones, who are standing. They're standing and they're hugging me. I think, "Hey it's my good friends *Catherine* and *Michael* hugging me," and this is just one too many meta-moments and I eject from my body, up hundreds of feet above the action, above Michael and Catherine and the hugs, like I'm at the end of a long string and I have a perfect, if distant, view of myself walking across the stage, shaking hands with Tom Hanks, approaching the microphone, saying something, saying something else. Time is passing. From my height, I think, "What is that person saying? Really, he better focus. He should reach into his pocket and pull out the hastily scribbled in-case-of-emergency 3x5 card with the people he'd like to thank."

I pull the card and stare down at it and realize it's blank. Blank? I think, "You always do this. A billion people watching and you've lost your homework." I look up and a huge monitor directly in my sightline is flashing TIME'S UP, TIME'S UP, TIME'S UP. I wing it, then I'm walking offstage with Tom Hanks and several tall blonde women. People are shaking my hand. Then there's Cameron Crowe winning for best original screenplay. Then I'm back in my seat hoping Steven wins for best director. And he does and I'm maybe even happier for him and we're hugging again and I'm wondering if I look as dazed as he does.

And later, I'm standing near Soderbergh and Spielberg as somebody says, "Hey, three Stevens" and as I'm thinking, "Yeah right," Barbara Boxer elbows me out of the way and takes my place and I watch their images flash frozen: Spielberg and Soderbergh smiling small smiles at each other with the tiny senator from California squeezed in diagonally at the edge of the frame.

Later, I'm at home with my family and I go back to work, reading the new script before I fall asleep. I work all the way back to Montreal. I work until I remember the day like a dream. Much later, when I'm back in town and he's back from shooting *Ocean's 11* in Las Vegas, Steven Soderbergh and I have dinner. He says, "Well, now we have the first lines of our obituaries," and then we talk of other things.

What It Feels Like to Win a Nobel Prize

[By James Heckman, 59, professor at the University of Chicago and winner of the 2000 prize for economics]

▶ I was in the shower at a hotel in Rio de Janeiro when I got the call. It was one of those rooms where there's a phone in the bathroom, so I was still dripping wet when I answered it. I immediately thought one of my students was playing a joke on me. I told the Swedish person on the phone, "This is a joke, isn't it?" Then the person said, "No, it isn't a joke." So I hung up and called my wife. Turns out the Swedes had called her, too, and she'd given them the number to my hotel room. And then it sank in that I'd just won the Nobel prize. I was overwhelmed, and still am. I got out of the shower and dried myself off. I sat down on the bed and looked out over the South Atlantic and thought to myself, "My God, my God."

In Stockholm, each laureate is assigned a stretch limousine, a driver, and an attaché. I'd never worn tails in my life and I had to wear them three times that week. I think the Swedes use more starch than most, because I felt like a true stuffed shirt. The receptions got very old, and there were a lot of them. They were very alien to the lifestyle I chose. I'm an academic and not a CEO or a diplomat. If there was an option to have the prize mailed to me, I would've taken it.

There's all this protocol and we had to practice the actual receipt of the award. You have to bow to the king, to the audience, and to the assembled academy. You're kind of like a penguin, bowing all the time. Beforehand, they gave us a movie to help us know what to expect. Pearl Buck was my favorite to watch. After she got her award, she never turned her back on the king and walked backwards up a flight of stairs. But I turned my back on the king. I wasn't that impressed. I wasn't nervous, either. It was more a sense of dread. All these receiving lines, and I'm meeting dukes, princes, counts and countesses. It seemed every Swede had about thirty medals. The Nobel prize itself is a big round disk with an estimated $15,000 worth of gold in it. I keep it in a safe. I have three brass replicas.

After the awards ceremony, there was this very formal dinner with many, many courses. Each course was announced with blowing bugles. The food was pretty good, but I'm not one to remember what we had. My wife remembers. They televise the event in Sweden. It's such a huge deal. People pack the streets and come to watch and look at our medals on display. We were treated like celebrities.

Back at home, people were looking for me to transform into some miniature Louis XIV, where I discard my academic functions and begin pontificating. I'm still the same person. And I believe my best work is ahead of me. But as they say, you're only as good as your latest paper.

—AS TOLD TO BRYAN MEALER

Part 4

What It Feels Like When Diseases Strike

What It Feels Like
TO HAVE AMNESIA

[By Mark Thistle, 37, co-owner of a car and van service]

▶ Amnesia is not like you see in movies. You remember 80 percent of what you need. It's the other 20 percent that ends up being totally critical.

It happened two years ago on a family skiing vacation. We were in Utah, at Snowbird. I was new to winter sports and decided to learn snowboarding. I'm not the most cautious person in the world. If I feel I understand something, I'll do it to the maximum I can possibly get away with. I was going down this huge hill, really going quite fast. No fancy stuff, no turns, just straight down the slope like a rocket. I don't remember precisely why I got tripped up. I do remember it happening very suddenly. And I'll tell you, having amnesia is just as interesting for what you do remember as what you don't. I remember my feet went out from under me and the back of my head hit the slope. I broke my fall with the back of my head. Not the best thing to do. And I remember thinking—I actually formed the sentence in my mind—"Wow: That's the hardest shot my head has ever taken!" And then, just like the movies, a black curtain comes down over my eyes.

The next thing I remember, a bunch of people are standing around me. My stuff is scattered all over the slope. My brother-in-law snaps a picture. The thing that most concerned me at the time was embarrassment. I felt that I was not injured. I just wanted everyone to go away. I don't remember getting back on my snowboard but I did. I snowboarded another couple hundred yards to a mid-slope lodge where we were all going for lunch. Then I remember sitting at a long table. Everyone in the family is talking and drinking something warm. I couldn't for the life of me remember where I was. I knew I was on a ski slope. I knew who these people were. I knew who I was. And I knew that I should know where I was. But I didn't. I had absolutely no idea where we were.

My head ached, like a regular little headache. I began to get a little scared. I began to understand that I was hurt, but I didn't want anyone else to know, not yet. I tried to marshal my inner resources. I thought to myself, "I can figure this out." I looked out the windows. There were huge mountains, the kind you never see in the eastern United States, so I figured I had to be in the West. And because everybody was speaking English, and there were no Canadian accents, I figured it was the western United States. I knew all that stuff, you know? So I said to myself, "Okay, what states are in the West?" And I'm naming all the states to myself— Vermont. Pennsylvania, California—but I couldn't remember what states were the western ones. I thought, "Okay, that's okay. So I can't remember where I am, let's try something easier, let's try to remember what time of year it is." And I knew it had to be winter; there was snow. I could name the months in order—January, February, etc. But I couldn't remember which ones were the winter months, you know?

So I was sitting there—my wife to my left, my in-laws, the whole family around me—and I became terrified. Even though I was thinking in complete sentences, I couldn't talk. I wanted to tell someone that something was wrong, but I couldn't form the words. Finally I said, "I don't feel good." I remember wanting to cry because I was afraid. I thought maybe this wasn't going to go away. That maybe this was very serious. It became clear now to everyone that I needed to get the rest of the way down the mountain. They handed me my snowboard; I realized I'd forgotten something else. I could not remember how to snowboard. But I had to get down the hill. I fell and I fell and I fell and I fell. All the way down the mountain. At some point, it all came back to me—I suddenly

recovered my ability to distinguish time and place. I didn't really mark the exact moment that it happened, but by the time I got to the bottom, it was all over. I knew where I was, what time of year it was, everything. It only lasted ninety minutes, but it was the scariest ninety minutes of my life. I spent the rest of the vacation in bed.

—AS TOLD TO MIKE SAGER

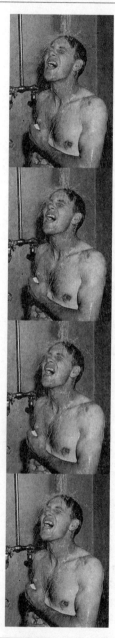

What It Feels Like TO HAVE AN OBSESSIVE-COMPULSIVE DISORDER

[By Craig Strobeck, 24, actor]

The moment I would get into the shower, I would feel exhaustion. I had to ready myself for between one and two and a half hours of shower time that I did not feel like doing, but I knew I had to, to stay clean. It would always start from top to bottom—from my head all the way down. Everything had its own specific ritual.

Washing my hair would take about an hour. I would wash the back of my hair, the sides of my hair, the front of my hair, the very top of my hair. Washing the front of my forehead, I would scrub it sixty times; it could never be sixty-one. Everything had to be an even amount of times. If I did anything an odd number of times, I'd have to do it all over again, despite how tired I might feel. After an hour, the hot water was gone. So 85 percent of the time, I was showering, doing the rest of my rituals in extremely cold water.

After the hair, I would do the shoulders, and I would have to scrub them to the point where I was scrubbing so hard on my collarbone and shoulder blades that it almost felt like the bone was piercing through the skin and touching the soap.

When it hurt like crazy, then I would know that I had completely scrubbed each area. I would run the soap up and down my arms at least one hundred to two hundred times each, just on the front side. I'd wrap the soap around my neck at least sixty to eighty times. Then I'd continue in this way down to my feet.

After I got out and dried myself off, I'd itch like crazy all over the place—my legs, my hands, my head itself. Sometimes after I was fully dressed, I would go back into the shower, sometimes in my clothes, sometimes I'd undress again, and just do one area that felt not clean enough. This voice in my head would speak to me, saying, "You're done, but I'd like you to do it again." There's this feeling in your mind like some terrible fate is going to meet you if you don't perform a certain ritual or task. Like you're trying to avoid paying your dues. The pressure to do it was constant and overwhelming. Like a voice saying, "Do not stop." Like a locomotive out of control.

—AS TOLD TO DANIEL TORDAY

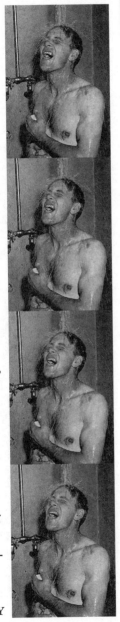

What It Feels Like to Have the Ebola Virus

[By Odong Walter, 32, shop owner, Gulu, Uganda]

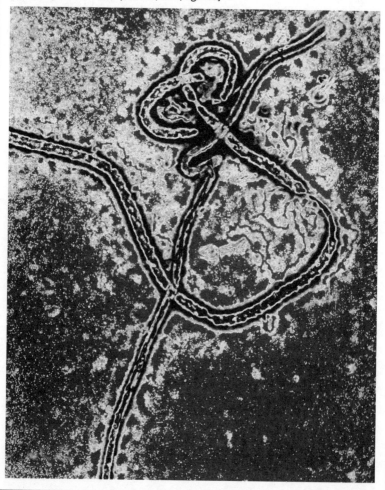

I can't tell you how I got Ebola. I can't tell you exactly. I never visited anybody in the hospital. I never tended to anyone with Ebola. I stayed in my shop, locked up. Some people think it comes from the heavens. Others think it is a poison. Here, we fear it as nothing else.

One morning in November, I woke up with a fever. I suffered with this fever for three weeks. In bed, I put on a shirt, a sweater, and a coat. And still it was too cold. I went to the hospital and was told I had severe malaria. But then the diarrhea started, and I was getting confused, shouting nonsense. There were terrible pains in my chest, too much pain.

When my stomach started to swell, they drew blood, and the tests came back positive for Ebola. In the isolation ward, I started bleeding. It was the first time I saw that much blood coming out of me. In ten minutes, a half liter of blood came from my nose. My stomach swelled so much that I could not raise myself to see it. The blood was also coming with the diarrhea. It was like a flooding river, and I was bleeding all over myself. Around me, people were vomiting blood, falling down, and dying immediately. I knew I was going to die, and I tried to write a will. I thought about my children. I regretted not doing enough for them.

I suffered like this for ten days. Courage made me survive.

Since my discharge from the hospital, I have constant, burning pain in my bones, especially in my legs. Noises bother me. I become so confused. I don't know what will happen to me. I may die in one year's time.

I feel very isolated. My mother and father have denied me. My wife denied me! My wife burned my things, broke the plates I had used. People fear me. When I walk down the street, they shout, "Ebola!" The children yell, "Ebola!" When I walk around my town, they call me Ebola.

—AS TOLD TO ANNIE SILVIO

What It Feels Like to Have a Severe STUTTER

[By Nate Benn, 24, clerk]

For 99 percent of the population, speaking is almost involuntary, like breathing. Most people don't have to think about the actual process. If they want to say something, the synapses fire, air is expelled, and the words flow. For me, it can be as hard as tackling William "The Refrigerator" Perry.

Some days it's so bad I can't say my own name. Nathan Benn. Seems like it should be easy, but it's not. So on days when it's really bad, I'll do an end-run around my tongue and switch to another name. When I introduce myself to someone that I'll never see again, I say Peyton instead of Nathan. Peyton? Because it sounds cool.

The thing is, there's a disconnect thing between my mind

and my tongue. My mind's processing a thousand words a minute, and the tongue is only squeezing out ten or twelve. I've been in and out of speech pathology offices since I was in the second grade, and they've taught me some good techniques. Relax your facial muscles and tongue, keep your eyes open, and keep breathing. But get me in front of a McDonald's drive-through window or on a date with a pretty girl, and I'm a mess. So I just have to power through, no matter how many times I repeat that syllable. When the word finally comes out, it's like a sneeze. Such a feeling of release, of relief.

There have been days when I didn't call anyone, or just gave one-word answers. But whenever I feel it's getting the best of me, I remember that I can sing without stuttering, and then gregariousness usually returns.

If living with a speech impediment has taught me anything, that is empathy. People have been able to look past my funny faces and twitches over the years, and see just another schmuck trying to communicate and be loved. Thus, I've learned to develop a mentality to not judge others on the surface. I'm obligated to show patience and tolerance to others, because the same has been done unto me. The Golden Rule pulls through once again.

What It Feels Like
TO HAVE AN EPILEPTIC SEIZURE

[By Taryn Drongowski, 23, student]

One gorgeous and rainy afternoon while I was studying at Oxford, I saw a dome of umbrellas. When I walked closer, I saw all these old British people clustered around a woman having a seizure. I could see myself in that scene. I thought, "Is that what it looks like when I have a seizure? Oh, my God." I saw this body convulsing; it just looked like somebody without a brain.

Before a seizure starts, I feel a weird tingling sensation, as if warm water were being poured over me. And I stop understanding what people are saying. I hear them, but it's all vowel sounds. I know that if I try to talk, it's going to be complete gibberish.

Then there's just an extreme tiredness. You're so exhausted, it's like a fever dream; all of your senses are messed up.

After that, you're actually seizing. Your mouth is opening and closing, opening and closing. You start in screaming, but your jaw won't stop chattering. Your tongue is totally relaxed in your mouth, so it kind of overlaps the bottom teeth, and you chew it up on the edges and in the front. Afterward, your mouth tastes like pennies, and your tongue is gnawed like a piece of meat that you can't quite bite through.

In the seizure, you lose control, body part by body part. That's the scariest, knowing it's happening, knowing, "I can't control this anymore." It's like being paralyzed, one body part at a time. You know the part of the brain that tells your arm to move, and you call to it, but the arm just won't move.

Then it's just like a light turning off.

—AS TOLD TO DANIEL TORDAY

What It Feels Like to Have Leprosy

[By Jose Ramirez, Jr., 55, social worker]

▶ I had just turned twenty when it was diagnosed. I didn't have any sensation in my arms. My feet and hands would swell up. I had high fevers, sometimes 105 degrees. Then I got what looked like pimples, these large, red nodules that wouldn't go away. They started out the size of a dime, but then spread and became much bigger, until they were the size of a lemon. They came up like a volcano and were filled with pus. When they burst, the pus came out and just settled, leaving a crater. And even though I lost sensation, there was still pain. I had sores on the bottoms of my feet and all over my body. My earlobes and testicles were swollen. Pretty soon, I was immobilized and could hardly walk.

At the time I was diagnosed, I'd been in the hospital for three days while they ran all kinds of tests. One day, some doctors, nurses, and my family all came and stood around my bed. Everyone was shrouded in caps, gowns, and gloves. It was like in the movies, when they find some kind of bacteria that is killing everybody—that's how they all appeared to me. Everyone wore these suits except my parents. They refused to put them on. Then this man from the Health Department came in from Austin and wanted to ask me a few questions. It was very embarrassing because he just focused on my nonexistent sex life. At the time they thought this disease was sexually transmitted. (My theory is that I got it from digging in infected soil in Texas.) When he finally noticed the puzzled look on my face, he stopped and said, "You mean they haven't told you what you have?" And I said, "No, I don't know." He didn't even tell me himself. He just handed me a blue pamphlet that said *Handbook for Patients with Leprosy*.

After he handed me that pamphlet, everything went dark. No color, just darkness. Those people shrouded in those caps and gowns no longer looked white—they were now black to me. It was as if my life had just ended.

My mother cried and cried. She apologized. She said she had committed some sins when she was young and that's why God was punishing her through me. But she never told me what those sins were. My birthday had just happened, but because of my illness, we hadn't celebrated. So my mother had gone out and bought a medal with the Virgin of Guadalupe on one side and San Juan on the other. It was a very tender moment. She put it over my neck. It was like a going-away present. She thought I was going to die. I still wear that medal.

I ended up in a facility in Louisiana that cared exclusively for leprosy patients. I stayed there for eight years. When I would leave the facility, people would point at me and whisper, "There goes the leper." One time, there was this guy peeing next to me in the bathroom. He saw me and his mouth came wide open. He turned white, his eyes were bulging, and he was peeing all over his pants. He was that afraid. He just ran off without zipping his penis back in his pants.

Now I educate people about the disease, explain that it's not communicable, how it can now be cured in a few months, and that noses and fingers don't really fall off.

I still have some craters on my leg. I still have no sensation in most of my legs, arms, and hands. I have to be very careful and check my shoes twice a day because, as recently as a month ago, I had a pebble there and I didn't know. It ended up causing a sore that became infected. I can cut myself and bleed for a long time and not know. When I was younger and I smoked, there were times when I burned my hand and didn't know until I smelled the flesh. I have a lot of scar tissue on my legs that is very dark. My face was luckily never affected because I got treatment in the right time. But I have almost no eyebrows and no body hair because the bacteria eats the hair follicle until it falls off.

—AS TOLD TO BRYAN MEALER

What It Feels Like
TO HAVE NARCOLEPSY

[By Melody Zarnke, 45]

▶ For a normal person to understand what narcoleptics feel like, they would have to forfeit sleep for forty-eight hours. That is how we feel every single day.

I was about twenty-one when I noticed I couldn't drive long distances without pulling over to nap. I thought I just needed more sleep, but it turned out to be the first indication that I had narcolepsy.

When a normal person goes to sleep they do not enter dream sleep for maybe 90 minutes after falling asleep. When narcoleptics like myself fall asleep we enter dream sleep right away. I am still awake when I begin to dream and I experience my dreams as hallucinations. Believe me, they are very, very real. If I dream that I got bit, I can feel it.

Sometimes I'll nod off and it's like an out-of-body experience. Other times it can happen during repetitive motion or while doing monotonous work and lasts only seconds. I don't even realize that anything has happened. Once I blacked out while I was laughing at a movie. My head rolled back and everything went dark and I wasn't able to return my head to the correct position without help from my husband.

They're getting close to a drug they hope can treat my condition. I'm not getting my hopes up but the thought of going to bed without fear is wonderful.

—AS TOLD TO KEVIN MCDONNELL

What It Feels Like to Be Albino

[By Craig Farraway, 37, musician]

Growing up hurt. They called me Whitey, Snow White, Milky. I just called people Brownie in return.

If I step out on a bright day, it looks like an overexposed picture. Everything is extremely washed out—and it can be painful, so I have to wear sunglasses. My eyes are blue, but there can be a red tinge to them because you're seeing the light bounce off my retina. Also, people with albinism have astigmatism and nystagmus—a movement of the eyes back and forth, vibrating really quickly.

About ten or fifteen minutes after being in direct sunlight, I start to sunburn—and my sunburns are three to four times worse than a normal person's. I feel like I'm cooked from the inside. I constantly have to wear sunscreen—40 SPF or higher.

Still, I love sunlight.

—AS TOLD TO DANIEL TORDAY

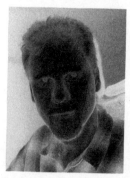

What It Feels Like to Have Tourette's Syndrome

[By Eric Heath, 43, marionette maker]

Having Tourette's is kind of like having a lightning storm going on inside your body. All of a sudden you'll just shout out a word. Or your whole body will whip to the side violently. You never know when it's going to strike.

It's a genetic thing; it was passed on to me by my family and kind of hung in the background until I was in my thirties. I was working at the Maryland Renaissance Festival selling pretzels one weekend and all of a sudden my arms were shooting up to the sky like I was a football official signaling a field goal.

Monkey!

naling a field goal. There was nothing I could do about it. It just happened.

I didn't want to limit myself because of this. So I continued to do things I'd been doing all along. I went to sing in a big concert choir along with a symphony orchestra. There

Toast!

were probably 150 of us on risers. I was in the middle, and of course I hadn't told anybody I had Tourette's syndrome. Once the lights went on and the music started, all the tension welled up in me and I jerked to the left, knocking a person off the end of the riser. I then came to the conclusion that standing shoulder to shoulder in a big group of people on risers is probably not a good idea.

You don't know whether what's about to come out is going to be physical or verbal.

Butter!

All of a sudden, I might just shout out, "Monkey!" Some people with Tourette's have coprolalia, which brings out swear words and obscenities. Their brains might get fascinated with the four-letter word that they just said and they'll have to say it a few more times, making the *f* really long or holding on to the *u*. Fortunately, most of the words that have come out of my mouth have been kind of goofy and nonoffensive. Aside from *monkey,* other words that have come out of my mouth have been *butter, toast,* and *boing.* Nobody usually pays attention to *butter* except waiters in restaurants. When the word *toast* kept coming out of my mouth at a friend's wedding, people who didn't know me said, "Good idea!" I've studied opera, so it's hard to go into stealth mode, especially when a huge operatic "Boing!" is coming out of my mouth.

There are times you get depressed and don't want to go out in public. But a lot of times people react to it wonderfully. When I shout, "Monkey!" they'll shout it back. It's as if they're saying,

Boing!

"Wow! I don't know why you just shouted 'Monkey!' but it made me feel good."

—AS TOLD TO CAL FUSSMAN

What It Feels Like
TO HAVE ANOREXIA

[By Gary Grah, 34, school counselor]

I finally accepted that I had a problem the second time I was hospitalized. That was in sophomore year of high school. I had lost almost 60 pounds and my weight was down to 94. When I checked into the hospital my body fat was either 0 or so close to 0 that they couldn't measure it. I remember them saying that my metabolism had started to burn muscle tissue and digest my organs as a source of energy. My pulse was at about 30 and my blood pressure was so low that it was the equivalent of somebody who was in shock.

I had induced anemia and was on the verge of pneumonia. They kept me in the hospital for 102 days, that time. The previous year, I had been in for 65 days.

Before going to the hospital, my routine at home was to get up at about 3:30 in the morning and exercise in my room for about four hours. Then I would have half a cup of cereal and half a cup of skim milk for breakfast and go to school. At lunch, I would eat maybe half an apple. When I got home from school, I would work out for another three hours and then have a light dinner. Then it was another two hours or so of working out, followed by homework, and another hour of calisthenics before going to bed at 10:30.

That was my life. This routine, the ritual of it, meant every-thing to me. When my parents were taking me to the hospital, I was arguing that I couldn't go because I had too many things to do—it was going to screw up my routine. Anorexia is maybe the only disease where you die of stubbornness.

I was excelling academically, doing fine in school sports, and because I never socialized with anyone, there was no question of drugs or alcohol. So there were none of the warning signs that a parent or a guidance counselor would usually pick up on that there was something wrong. With all of that, plus the fact that the change is very gradual, you'd be surprised how many people you can fool and how long you can fool them. It was when my weight dropped below 100 pounds and I looked like a skeleton that my parents insisted on having me evaluated, and the hospital staff insisted that I be admitted that day. All these professionals are taking one look at me and they know instantly that I need help—but as crazy as it sounds, I still thought I looked fat. I would see myself in the mirror and the first thing that would come into my head was how much farther I still had to go before I reached my goal. I guess the goal was being dead, although I wasn't admitting that to myself at the time.

At the hospital, they would make me eat and because I was such a manipulative people-pleaser, I would do it. Mostly, I would do it. About a third of what they gave me I would shove down my pants or hide in my socks. They also wouldn't let me exercise, but it took only a week or so to figure a way around that. I got one of those traveler's alarm clocks that you can set to vibrate, instead of ringing. I watched the night nurses for a week or so and figured out when they changed shifts and when they made their rounds.

I would set the alarm for 2:15 and know that I had forty-five minutes when I could do pushups and situps without being caught, and then still have enough time to get back in bed and slow my heart rate down so that when they checked me at 3:30, nothing would seem strange. Then I'd set the alarm for 4:15 and do the same thing all over again.

In the hospital, all I could think about was exercise and killing myself. I wanted to die, but I needed to work out first. I was a perfectionist and I felt like I didn't deserve to live unless I was hurting myself by over-training, dieting, and depriving myself of sleep. The more pain I was in, the better I felt about myself.

By the time I got out of the hospital, my weight was back up in the 130s. Not great, but I was out of danger. I wasn't out of the woods, though. I went back into the hospital four more times over the next four years. The last time, when I was a sophomore in college, I finally turned a corner. I gave up on trying to be perfect. I stopped trying to kill myself in slow motion.

—AS TOLD TO MATTHEW FENTON

Part 5

What It Feels Like to Battle the Unknown

What It Feels Like

TO HAVE MULTIPLE PERSONALITIES

(Dissociative Identity Disorder)

[By Rachel Downing, 58, clinical social worker]

When I was a child I experienced having different personalities as magic. If I was frightened, I could shut my eyes and all the scared feelings would go away. And I'd open my eyes and everything would be normal again.

In 1976 my father died. I became physically ill, but the doctors could not find anything wrong with me. They sent me to a therapist who specializes in psychosomatic medicine. I was suicidal, and I said to him, "That's it. I'm killing myself. There's no reason to go on." And I curled up in this big blue chair in his office and I wouldn't talk, and he said to me, "Rachel, you can't come to my office, tell me you have a gun and want to kill yourself, and not talk to me. You have to talk to me, Rachel." And this little voice said, "I'm not Rachel." And he said, "Who are you?" And the response, in a childlike voice, was, "I'm the little girl." And he said, "Little girl, what can you tell me about yourself?" And she said, "My daddy was mean to me." And that really opened the door.

My father was an Episcopal minister so I had to be nice and smile at church and appear happy. One reason for having the different personalities is the abuse, but the other is because you have to live different lives, so you develop these dissociated parts of yourself. My therapist and I realized later that there were hundreds of them.

Most of my personalities had functions. There were personalities that went to school and personalities that played in the house. The part of me that handled feelings of shame and inadequacy called herself Shela. When I was in that personality, I remember, I used to stutter. Karlina was a protective personality

Shela

that would scare people away by being angry and explosive. I even incorporated my father as a personality, and I would speak like him and say things like, "I'm in charge of her life. I can do whatever I want." There was another one—a childlike personality—that just called herself "the puppy."

I would often feel dizzy and a little off balance when I was about to shift and sometimes I would have feelings of fear—I would be afraid

The Puppy

that I wouldn't be able to remember that my name was Rachel. I would think, "Oh my

God, what if I can't remember my name? What if I get stopped by the police and tell them I'm somebody else?"

I had one personality within me that was the late-night girl and appeared at one and two and three in the morning, so I took my middle name, Anne, and the L sound from *late night*, and made it Leanna— that's how she got her name. Leanna—that part of me—was very religious and very spiritual. She viewed the personalities as sheep and herself as the shepherdess. And she loved all the personalities and she went to them and brought them to therapy and she was not afraid of any of them, even the ones that were suicidal or harmful to myself. She wanted to make sure that every sheep was brought home. She became the internal bridge between all the parts of myself.

Leanna

I integrated all of my personalities in 1990. I stopped referring to myself in the third person. When I'd feel myself on the edge of dissociating into another personality, I'd just say, "I'm not going to allow this to happen." I began to realize that I was addicted to it, like an alcoholic.

Sometimes people who have DID don't want to integrate their personalities. They say, "I don't want to kill them off." They worry that they are going to lose something. Well, I have news for them, you don't lose anything. You keep them all—they're all sides of you. It's so much better to be a whole person.

—AS TOLD TO TOM COLLIGAN

What It Feels Like
TO UNDERGO AN EXORCISM

[By Kellie, 27, assistant director]

▶ We call it a deliverance, not an exorcism. Besides me, there were four other people in the room—two pastors and two women—praying over me and commanding the spirits to leave. One of the women, June, stayed face-to-face with me the whole time. She had the ability to sense the presence of evil—and she read my face. From what I understand, you could see it in my eyes.

I saw things. And I smelled things, too. There was a sulfuric, acidic, burning smell. When I smelled it, I looked to the right, and I saw something. I can't even describe what it was, but it was horrible. June saw it, too.

I remember freaking out and asking her, "What is that?" And she said, "It's okay, it's okay." And then it left. At times I became violent. When the pastor commanded a spirit to leave, I would feel it rise up within me, and I would want to bolt. I would want to hurt someone, want to hurt myself. I would bang my head against the floor. But it wasn't me. I couldn't control myself at all.

That first session started at ten in the morning and lasted until after eight at night. I had three more sessions over the next few months before God delivered me.

Before this all started, I was ornery as all get-out. But as time passed, I started to feel different. It was like my heart had a little shell around it, and we were breaking off the pieces. Still, it's an ongoing battle. We all need deliverance, every day.

—AS TOLD TO BRENDAN VAUGHAN

What It Feels Like
TO PERFORM AN EXORCISM

[By June Christopher, 39, nurse]

With Kellie, we were up against some powerful evil.

When you're in the room with evil there is a heaviness, an atmospheric heaviness. It's almost like something is sitting on you, but you can't see it. You feel nauseated. You have a headache. You feel edgy, irritable, and sometimes you get this urge to just *get out of the room*.

I work with a woman named Lisa who also has the gift of discernment. Occasionally I'll see a cloud of black smoke drift through the room, and we'll say to each other, "Did you see that?" That happened two or three times during Kellie's deliverance. But with the gift of discernment also comes the ability to sense the presence of angels, the presence of the Lord. At one point during Kellie's deliverance we took a break, and the whole room sort of lit up with fireflies, bright lights all above, and I knew the Lord was revealing to me that although we were resting, he was still fighting. It was very encouraging.

At the end of that first session, we had a feeling we weren't finished. But there was only so much that she could take, and we could take, in one day. We knew that what was harassing Kellie was gonna fight back. It's a war. It's a war, and we're the prizes, and they don't like to lose. So we knew it was gonna take some time.

—AS TOLD TO BRENDAN VAUGHAN

Part 6

What It Feels Like to Have an Extreme Body

What It Feels Like to Be Really, Really Tall

[By Shawn Bradley, 31, 7'6" center, Dallas Mavericks]

▶ So here's how my day starts—I get up in the morning, and as I go to the bathroom I have to duck through the first door. I have to duck as I go into the closet. I have to duck down to see the mirror in our room, I have to duck down for the shower. The shower hits me in the middle of the chest. I can't fit in the tub—I have to go into the swimming pool if I want to be completely submerged. I have a specific way to get in the car—my right knee goes in first, around the steering wheel, then I slide in. Call me a contortionist if you will.

I remember in high school I was 7'6" already, and we were in an opponent's locker room. I could see over the top of all the lockers, and it was disgusting—it was dusty, and there were empty drink bottles, and articles of clothing that had been discarded up there and were lost forever. And my coach, who was about 6'4", stood on one of the benches so we could see eye to eye. He said, "You live in a dirty world, don't you?" And I said, "Yeah, it's dusty and dirty." Even in people's homes, if I have to duck through the doorway, there's dust on top of the molding. The tops of fridges are never clean.

When I was a kid and I'd go out with my parents to a mall or something, I was the place that you'd meet at. Everyone knew where I was. They'd say, "Meet at Shawn." I was never shorter than anyone my age. When I was in third grade, they used to make me play with people who were in sixth grade because I was their size rather than their age. They made me play with people my size.

All the clothes that I get pretty much have to be custom-made. I only wear a size 17 shoe, which is not that big, but I still have to special-order those. I wear a 42 inseam. I don't ever find shirts that are long enough. I have to get a sleeping bag made special, get a really big tent for when we go camping.

The only place I can sit on an airplane is first class, and even that's cramped. Occasionally there'll be an exit door that won't have a seat in front of it, and I can fit there. Last year when I was going from Germany to Turkey, there was absolutely no room. It was physically impossible for me to sit in the seat and get a seat belt around me. The flight attendant and I switched seats and I had to sit in the jump seat. The flight attendant told me several things to do in the case of an emergency, and I was a flight attendant for the day.

The bed I have now is about 9 feet long, and it's a little too long for my bedroom. The one I have on order is 8 feet long. That seems to be the perfect size for us. I grew up my whole life with my feet hanging off the bed, and I'm kind of used to that.

If there's something on the top shelf my wife needs, while she's getting ready I can get it for her, no problem—she's only 5'3". When I'm in a crowd, I can see all the bald spots. I've really never met anyone taller than me, but I've had dreams of meeting people that are taller than me.

—AS TOLD TO DANIEL TORDAY

What It Feels Like to Be Really, Really Really Short

[By Gabriel Pimentel, 24, 2'11" actor]

People are always staring at me. I guess I understand why: I'm 2'11", which is really short. Technically, I'm a dwarf, because all the parts of my body are in the right proportions, but the term you're supposed to use is "little person." I really don't care what anyone calls me as long as they don't say, "You're so cute!" I hate that. Cute is for babies or toy poodles. That's why I work out. I weigh only 54 pounds, but I can bench-press 110. I'm like a little pit bull.

Being small was tough growing up. But I was lucky because Billy Barty once visited my school and pulled out a diamond and showed it to everyone and said, "This is really, really small, but it's extremely valuable." After that, everyone treated me better.

Still, it's not easy. Every little thing that people take for granted is a workout for me. If I want to get something from a cabinet, I have to hop up onto a chair and then onto the counter like a monkey. I always have to use handicapped bathrooms so I can use the support railings to balance myself while I stand on the toilet edge and do my business. When I'm in an elevator, I have to jump as high as I can to hit the button if I'm going to a high floor. If I go to the movies, I fold my leg under myself and sit on it. If I'm involved with a woman, my face usually spends a lot of time in the middle of her belly. The only thing that's not difficult is clothes shopping. I go to the Gap. It's funny—they always have clothes in my size.

But it's kinda cool being short. I bill myself as "the Shortest Guy in L.A." and have done some movies and music videos. I'd like to be the Al Pacino or Robert De Niro of little people, but it's tough in Hollywood. They think little people can only be used for laughs. But we can be tough like anyone else. We can be mad. We can be sad.

—AS TOLD TO GERSH KUNTZMAN

What It Feels Like to Weigh 400 Pounds

[By Norris Chumley, 46, author of the book and video The Joy of Weight Loss]

There was no space between my legs. I got all sorts of infections. My legs always had boils. Arms, too. Boils, pimples, rashes under the arms, on the chest. I had a 68-inch waist. I had a 25-inch neck—the size of a color TV. I wore a size 14 EEEEE width shoe. I had to special-order everything.

It was uncomfortable to lie down because it was hard to breathe. I could only sleep on my back, and I had to prop myself up with four or five pillows, sort of sitting halfway up. In the morning I had to roll over to one side, sort of sit up and lean, and then roll myself off the bed.

For breakfast, I had a huge bowl of cereal, as sugary as possible: Lucky Charms, Cocoa Krispies. Then an Egg McMuffin, preferably two Egg McMuffins, hash browns, extra-large hot chocolate. And then two hours later I'd have two or three candy bars: Snickers, Three Musketeers. I would always have stuff available, like Hostess Fruit Tarts—preferably cherry—or 1-pound bags of M&M candies. I had no idea what it meant to not be hungry. When I'd get off the phone, I'd go have something to eat. When it was time to go to bed, I had to have half a pint or half a gallon of ice cream or I couldn't get to sleep. And I would drop everything in my life to get it. A heroin addict has to have a fix; I had to have ice cream.

Right: Norris Chumley in 1974, before his weight loss. Photo: Robert Baldridge

All the way through high school, I couldn't sit at a normal desk, so I'd just sit on a regular chair and put my books and my notebook on my lap. I was the only kid in school who had to do that. And I had to be really careful where I sat down, because many times I would break chairs. Once I went on a job interview and the guy took me out to lunch at a restaurant that had metal, bent-frame chairs shaped like an *S*, so there wasn't any support in the back.

When I sat down I could feel the metal frame bending, so I bent forward on my thighs for an hour and a half. The second that I sat back—BOOM!—the chair broke; I snapped the metal frame and landed on my back. It took like four people to pull me up. There were about two hundred people in the restaurant. I think the job interviewer was as upset and embarrassed as I was. His face turned all colors of red, but he called me the next day and hired me anyway. A very kind and understanding boss, that's for sure.

I would no longer go see movies or plays because I had to stuff myself into the seats. I had to pick up my gut, take a deep breath, and plop down into the seat. Then I'd let it go, but imagine all that extra skin that had been pulled up blobbing over the chair and even onto the person next to you. Because there's so much fat around you, you can't completely sit back, so you're kind of on the edge of your seat for an hour and a half. Just imagine you have a rubber inner tube around you all the time. Try to sit down in a rubber inner tube. It's in the way.

I had to sit down to tie my shoes. I couldn't bend over. It would take a half hour to cut my toenails. I avoided going to the bathroom. I would hold it all day long. I didn't want to reveal myself. I didn't go into a locker room and change clothes until I was thirty-two years old.

When I lost all this weight, I had expanded my skin so

much that it wouldn't shrink back. I had an apron of excess skin that went down to my knees. After two years of daily exercise programs, I decided to cut the fucking shit off. It was causing all sorts of skin rashes and infections. The plastic surgeons removed 4 square feet of excess skin from my stomach and chest. I could've made a set of luggage with my excess skin.

That was my life twenty years ago, before I lost 160 pounds. I thank God for the opportunity to recover the life that I was cheated out of from being so fat.

—AS TOLD TO MATT CLAUS

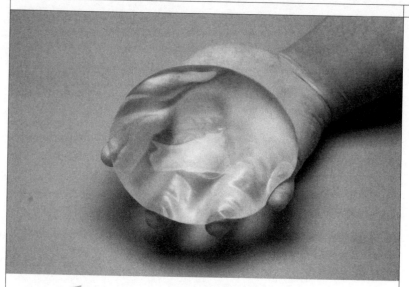

What It Feels Like to Touch Fake Boobs

[By Julian Kaye, 41, real estate broker]

▲ They feel like grapefruits. You know the way a grapefruit gives when you push on it, but you can't really squeeze it because it's firm? They feel like that. Or you could say it's like a muscle. Like a good, hard bicep, only in front. My wife was turning thirty-seven. She was concerned that gravity was taking hold. I assured her that wasn't the case. I told her to try pushups. But she kept on. The surgery was done, which took her from a 34B to a 36C. They're heavier. They have weight. But I'll tell you, they looked amazing. The morning after the surgery, she got up out of bed and it was like a phoenix rising.

—AS TOLD TO DANIEL TORDAY

What It Feels Like to Have Fake Boobs

[By Ivana, 25, model and actress]

Growing up, my sister always had a chest, and I had nothing. It always was important to me—I don't know why, exactly—and as soon as I made up my mind to get implants there was no turning back. I didn't do it for anyone else or my job; breasts were just something I'd wanted my whole life—well, since puberty, anyway.

When I got out of surgery, I just couldn't wait to look down. The first time I saw my chest, it was weird because they were a lot bigger than I thought they'd be, because they get really swollen at first. So I was thinking, "Whoa—what did I do?" But the swelling went down within a month. In the end, I went from an A cup to a C cup.

I was actually surprised that there wasn't much pain. When I first got them, I remember it felt like I'd worked out way too much. Like I had really really sore muscles from exercising. You can't lift heavy things or anything like that, but I was fully functioning the day of my surgery. It does feel weird to have something foreign in your body, though. Lying down, especially. It's still kind of awkward sometimes. Like if I lie down on my stomach, it feels like, "Wait? Something's not quite right in here?" because the implants don't give like the rest of your body. It doesn't feel like I'm propped up or anything. And it doesn't feel like you're lying on little base-balls or anything—my implants aren't hard, even though some that are huge look stiff. It's more awkward than anything, like having little pillows under your chest when you're not used to it. If people who sleep with one pillow under their head suddenly switched to three, it would feel weird—but not painful, you know? Just different.

Since my implants aren't that big, they don't feel like basketballs, or even like melons or anything, when you touch them. It's more like water balloons that aren't completely full. And sometimes when you touch them, you can feel the liquid inside, too, which I guess is weird. Sometimes, when I bend over, I can feel the liquid moving around inside the implants, too, and that's strange.

My whole self-image changed. Within a week I booked some of the biggest modeling jobs I'd ever done. I know it's not all about my chest, either—it's just how I felt about myself. I had more confidence after the procedure, and people can see that.

—AS TOLD TO ELIZABETH EINSTEIN

What It Feels Like
TO CHANGE FROM A MAN TO A WOMAN

[By Karyn Kent, 48, marketing professional]

I was probably six years old when I first dressed up. I did it maybe once a month and progressed into makeup when I got into my teens. I would go out walking the streets and sometimes people would spot me. There was an incredible adrenaline rush because I was afraid of being discovered by my parents or anyone in the world for that matter.

By the time I got into college, I went into a period of complete remission. Eventually I met somebody and got married. My wife had no clue. But in the tenth year of our marriage, my wife caught me in the middle of the night, playing around cross-dressing in another room. We'd just had our first child. She was devastated. We were living in Los Angeles at this point, and by that time, I was just on the tip of realization that I was a transsexual. I was about forty-two years old. Eventually, my wife and I divorced. I began to plan my transition, which is the first step prior to surgery. I formulated a letter and sent it out to everyone at work. I gave them a month notice before full transition. It was kind of confusing for everybody because they didn't know how to even address me anymore.

I lived almost a year as a woman before having the surgery. I'd had plenty of practice by that point, so I was probably better off than most transsexuals. It's not like I look like a man in a dress.

During transition, I started dating the man who's now my husband. He actually came with me to the surgery, which I had in Thailand. The technical term is *penile inversion*. After waking up from surgery, I felt a lot of pain, but not a horrific amount. You wake up and you have this big cast made of bandages. The cast is packed in, and when they start pulling it out, it's not the most pleasant feeling in the world. They use the existing tissue. Your nerve endings and bundles are actually preserved. That's what's used to give you sen-

sation in the clitoris area. I have a clitoris. Aesthetically, a gynecologist wouldn't even know unless they really started looking inside.

It took me about two months to fully heal. Three months until I was feeling totally back to normal, where I could sit on a bicycle. I had to get a little inflatable rubber doughnut to sit on for about six weeks. The area was really tender. There were still some sutures that would dissolve over a period of time.

I can have sex and orgasm. It's functional in that way. The orgasms are different, though. The male has this orgasm and that's basically it. For a female, it's more of an ongoing thing during the course of intercourse, more of a whole-body experience. As opposed to men—men have sex like dogs.

As far as growing breasts, I took hormones. It's really not much different than what any teenage girl goes through. I noticed an overall smoothness to my skin first, then sensitivity to the breasts as development started. After about four years of gradual growth my development seemed to be mostly over. Emotionally you get a dose of mood swings mixed with insecurity—it's like going through puberty all over again.

I didn't really have too much of an issue with my Adam's apple, but I did opt for a small surgery called a thyroid cartilage reduction to help reduce any telltale signs. That surgery was done at the same time as the other and was virtually painless.

One fundamental thing is that females communicate on a vastly different level than men. A lot of it is unspoken. You walk into a room with other women and you can sense what they're sensing. It's almost telepathy. Either you get it or you don't. Luckily I got it.

For myself, I was totally heterosexual before, and I'm totally heterosexual now. I didn't change. I didn't become homosexual. Being with a guy feels much more natural. The thought of being with a woman doesn't do much for me. But that's just me.

—AS TOLD TO BRYAN MEALER

What It Feels Like
TO CHANGE FROM A WOMAN TO A MAN

[By Daniel K., 35, grad student]

As a kid, it's not that I wanted to be a boy; I was already a boy. Except unfortunately I wasn't born with the parts. I remember I would go to the boys' room to pee in nursery school, and would try to pee standing up. I played boys' basketball and Little League. I was lean and muscular with a little Dutch boy haircut.

I have always been sexually attracted to women. In high school I was involved with the homecoming queen. She was straight and had always dated men. In college I was also involved with several other heterosexual women. But I never dated lesbians. Right before my transition, I worked at a Fortune 500 company, and people kept telling me how it was so great that I was this successful female. They would say, "You're a cute girl." I would always have people tell me I looked like Eddie Van Halen. Strange, but I didn't mind that.

It was three years ago when I received my first shot of testosterone. I'll take this the rest of my life. The T heightens the libido. I'm also hairier. I'm growing facial hair and have to shave. I'm kind of close to getting a goatee. I've had two surgeries. One was chest surgery. I was lucky that I wasn't a large-breasted woman. For them, it's basically a mastectomy and deep scars are left. For me, they just went around the nipple area, scooped the stuff out, then sewed it back up. I also had a hysterectomy, had everything taken right out.

I think someday I'll have the surgery to have a penis, but I'm waiting on them to get better at the procedure. With the testosterone, the clitoris grows and it starts to look like you literally have a penis. This is what has happened with me. That in itself can be frustrating, because you know something is down there, but you're limited with it. Some have more growth than others, but you can't get hard enough to penetrate.

I used to be anxious about going to the men's room and going to

a stall to sit down and pee. When I walk out, I was worried guys would say, "Dude, what's wrong?" But no one stares at your parts in the men's room and no one really pays attention.

There's this guy at work who I goof with all the time. A big Italian guy. He punches me and I punch him, just goof off a lot. He doesn't know about my transition. And I feel uncomfortable, not because I don't feel as real or as manly as him, but I don't ever want to be misleading anyone. But then again, it's not safe for me to go around saying, "Howya doin? I'm Dan and I'm a transsexual." When I went out for my hysterectomy, he didn't know why I was absent from work. He thought I had a hernia or something. He called me over to him and said, "You gonna be all right, buddy?" and I said, "Yeah, I'll be okay," then he kinda whispered, "You're not gonna have a sex change on me, are ya?" That was pretty funny.

—AS TOLD TO BRYAN MEALER

What It Feels Like to Starve

[By Laurence McKeown, 46, former Irish Republican Army political prisoner]

In Ireland, through the centuries, a hunger strike was always regarded as an honorable thing. If someone was to fast at your door because you had done them injustice, it was the most dishonorable thing that could be done to you. In 1981, we were between a rock and a hard place. We could either accept the status of being normal criminal prisoners or embark on a hunger strike to gain status as political prisoners.

I was one of many to volunteer. I received communication from the IRA council on the outside while at Sunday mass. It was written on a small piece of cigarette paper wrapped in plastic that had been smuggled in. It said, "Comrade, you have volunteered to embark upon a hunger strike. Are you aware that this means you will most likely be dead in two months? Rethink your decision." For me, there was no rethinking. I was twenty-four years old.

All we could consume was water and salt so our bodies would perform their normal functions. We dipped our finger in salt and put it into our mouth about six times a day. We drank at least six pints of water so our kidneys and liver were flushed. Your body fared a lot worse if you had a lot of fat. It burned up the fat before it ate the muscle, and the fat burns with a very toxic residue that puts your kidneys under a lot of pressure. At the time, I was $10\frac{1}{2}$ stones (147 pounds), already thin from bad prison food.

The first few days, you always feel hungry. But you know you're not going to eat, so it's an emptiness rather than a hunger. After that, your stomach shrinks, so you don't even have the empty feeling. By drinking water, you can make the stomach think there's something in it.

I was moved to the prison hospital after twenty-one days. By then I was a lot weaker and walked a lot slower. If I got out of bed too quickly, I got dizzy and nauseous.

We would all sit and watch the television and the adverts would come on about food; we would joke about what we would eat when the hunger strike was over. At the time, I had never tasted Indian curry, but I had heard about it in jail and was fascinated by it at that stage.

The food actually got better during the strike. It was very warm and the plates were spilling over. At each mealtime, that food sat there until the grease congealed and the smell became obnoxious. When you're on a hunger strike, your sense of smell becomes very sharp, even as hearing and vision fail. Once, we asked them to stop using the floor polish because the smell was making us nauseated.

I was getting more gaunt and the flesh was dropping off around my shoulders. The temples and cheeks became sunken and the head looked narrow and shrunken. The collarbone became exposed and my hips disappeared into bones. My spine and ribs became very prominent. Blood vessels started to break down in the arms and face; I could see small blue marks under the skin where they had burst.

At forty days the vision goes. First, I got blurred and double vision, then a mix of the two. Finally I got to the point where I didn't want my eyes open because everything was blurred.

During the last days, we were lying on sheepskin rugs and they were rubbing us down with cream every day to stop the skin from breaking. I didn't really experience pain, but people did get sick and throw up all the time. I had nothing to throw up but green bile. It took a toll on the body because all I could do was retch. That happened to me at sixty-six days.

I urinated because we were drinking a lot of water. We discovered later that during the last stages of someone's strike, everyone had a bowel movement, which was a very painful experience. Whenever this happened to someone, they generally died within two or three days. At sixty days, this happened to me. I went to the toilet for about two hours. It was very dramatic and painful and felt like it was ripping my insides apart. People would scream because it took so long. After it happened, I was helped back to my cell and didn't get out of bed after that.

Families were let in once the conditions were critical, and after sixty-eight days, my family was let in to see me. My father, brother, and sister asked me to come off the strike, and I said that I wouldn't. My mother said to me, "You know what you have to do and I know what I have to do." At the time I didn't understand what she meant, but after I slipped into a coma, she authorized medical intervention. It was the morning of the seventieth day.

They took two large syringes full of vitamins and injected me in each leg. I was then taken to a hospital in Belfast and hooked up to drips. Between the two, I was able to regain consciousness that evening. I weighed 7 stones (98 pounds). When I woke up I heard a woman's voice, a very friendly voice, and she was using my first name. No one in prison ever used my first name. I remember her hands touching me, and it was a caring touch, not a brutal one. Later I was moved into a military hospital a few miles away. I remember lying in bed and hearing children playing. Their ward was near mine, and I realized that it was the first time in five years that I had heard children.

I went back to prison three weeks later and the hunger strike was still happening. I could hardly see and had to hold on to walls in order to walk. I got nauseated if I stood for too long. Three days later, the hunger strike was called off.

—AS TOLD TO BRYAN MEALER

Part 7

What It Feels Like When People Attack

What It Feels Like to Get Shot in the Head

[By Laura Elena Harring, 38, actress, star of Mulholland Drive]

▶ I'm twelve years old at the time, and my mom and stepfather take me and my sisters to the movies in San Antonio. We're driving through the parking lot, and I'm craning my head out the window looking for the cinema. There are two cars behind us. Suddenly, one of them screeches off and someone in the other car starts shooting. We hear three loud bangs, but I only hear two because the second one hits me in the head. It feels like my head was hit with a rock from a slingshot. My stepfather yells, "They're gunshots! Get down!" and I say, "I think they hit me." I immediately put my head down into my mother's lap. She grabs my white sweater and starts pressing down. And all I can hear is blub blub, blub blub from the blood running down my face. It's very warm. Everything is going part in slow motion, part in fast motion. There's this low-pitched ringing in my head—naaaaaaaa—and my mother is saying Hail Marys in Spanish.

My sister peeks over the seat and sees all the blood. She crinkles her face and opens her mouth like that painting *The Scream*. It's the scariest face I've ever seen. She lets out a shriek that gets my other sisters crying. That's when I think, "I'm going to die."

At the hospital, I'm on a cart and my parents are above me running with the doctors. The coating of blood is so heavy and thick on my face that I can't open one eye or my mouth. I have long, dark hair, and they shave off half of it. They take X rays but can't find the bullet. Turns out the bullet hit the side of my head, then continued on to the rearview mirror. Later my stepfather found it crushed on the floorboard. The doctor said it missed my brain by a millimeter.

—AS TOLD TO BRYAN MEALER

What It Feels Like
TO BE HELD HOSTAGE

[By Barry Rosen, 59, former press attaché at the American embassy in Tehran, held by the Iranians for 443 days in 1979–80]

I was in my office in the beautiful American embassy compound in Tehran when a hundred club-wielding Iranian men and women climbed over the walls. Before I knew it, several young terrorists were holding Kalashnikovs to my head and yelling that I was a spymaster.

I spent the first weeks tied to a chair, blindfolded, transferred from one dark and dingy place to another. They'd throw you in a truck and drive you around and you didn't know where they were taking you. I finally ended up in a maximum-security prison where I could hear the screams of dissident Iranians being tortured. I spent most of the time trying to stave off depression. If there was a light ray coming in from the window, I would spend three hours following that as it moved down the wall. Every day, I'd walk six miles in my cell in a figure-eight pattern. One time, someone sent me and my cellmates the boating section of the *Washington Post,* and every day, we'd pick a different boat from the classifieds and go sailing on the Potomac in our minds.

I didn't want to be friendly with any of my captors. They asked me, "When this is over, can you get me a visa to America?" I said, "If you ever come to the United States, I'll kill you." But after awhile, I gave up being defiant because it only got me struck over and over again. I kept relations very formal.

I was in my underwear most of the time. I slept on a foam rectangle. I had a thin blanket, but no sheets. For food, we'd have Iranian bread and a soupy thing with a little meat in it. To show us their supposed sense of humanity, they once gave us a glass of grapefruit juice.

I had a difficult time sleeping. I didn't really sleep for months. I'd fear subconsciously that I would die if I fell asleep, so I would wake up. I tried to think about the positive. I tried to think about my family.

When we finally got released, we weren't used to the outdoors. It was so bright, I couldn't focus well for weeks.

—AS TOLD TO GERSH KUNTZMAN

What It Feels Like to Be a Mob Hit Man

[Name withheld, 52, former associate, major crime family, New York City; former protectee, federal Witness Security Program]

It's nerve-racking. Don't let anyone tell you any different. Anybody who's any good at this is concentrating with every nerve in their body, trying to get it done right and trying not to get caught. The first time I was supposed to do the work, my Uncle Rich, who was a captain with one of the big families, tells me to get ready. I'm thinking it's a soldier from another family they have a problem with, maybe somebody from my uncle's crew who's a weak link, something like that. Not even close.

Turns out it's a guy I used to go to school with. His name was Matty. He had wised off to my uncle twelve years earlier. By that time he was just out of high school and I was already in the Army, so I wasn't in touch with him anymore. Anyway, he had looked at my uncle's sister funny on the street, or something like that. My uncle told him to fuck off, and the guy broke his nose. For this, he's going to die.

Uncle Rich finds out that this guy is in an all-night craps game on Bath Avenue, in Brooklyn. It's in the back of a bar. He calls Freddie, who worked for my uncle. A real idiot, but a stone killer. And Freddie has a stash of every kind of weapon you can think of: shotguns, machine guns, swords, hatchets. And my uncle decides that a hand grenade is what makes the most sense. Don't ask me how he came up with that. But sure enough, Freddie has some hand grenades. And we're going to rig a hand grenade to go off when this guy opens up the door to his car.

It's about one in the morning when we find his car. I tell Freddie and my uncle to stand watch about 30 feet from either end of the car. The problem is that this bar is right down the block from the 62nd Precinct house. I keep telling my uncle that another night would be better. What sense does it make to rig a bomb in a car 100 yards from a precinct full of cops? But no, it's gotta be tonight. Twelve years and my uncle can't wait another week.

I jack my way into the car and I go to work. I'm sitting in the front passenger seat and I latch a fishhook with about 18 inches of line around the base of the lock button on the driver's-side door. The idea is that when the door opens, the line will pull. Then I run fishing line from that hook down to where I'm going to stash the grenade, which is between the seat and the back rest. I jam the grenade into this space and tie the fishing line around the inside of the lever.

Now I unpin the grenade. The pressure of being stuck between the seat and the back rest keeps the lever pushed down. But when the door opens, the fishing line is going to yank the grenade out from between the seat and the back rest and the lever is going to flip up. Five seconds later, it's showtime. This is a concussion grenade, not the fragmentation kind, so he won't be killed by shrapnel. But Freddie the expert keeps telling us that that blast is strong enough to tear this guy in half.

I lock the doors from the inside and get out the front passenger-side door. Then I jam toothpicks into the other three doors, to make sure that Matty can't screw things up by getting in anywhere but the front left door. So we're all set. Now Freddie and my uncle decide to go home and get some sleep, but I'm too keyed up for that. Too many things can go wrong. I get my car and drive to a spot around the corner from where Matty's car is parked. From where I'm parked, I can't see his car directly, but I'll definitely be able to hear the blast.

So it's almost 5:30 and I hear a sound like a stick of dynamite going off inside a metal Dumpster and I know my trap worked. But the punchline is that the blast was strong enough to blow Matty right through the roof of his car and clear across the street and break his leg. But not enough to kill him.

A year later, Uncle Rich and Freddie killed Matty. They shot him in the street, outside of another craps game. I was there, as backup, but I didn't do the shooting. My uncle died about six years later. Natural causes, old age. I hadn't seen him for awhile, because by then, I was in the witness protection program. But about a year before Uncle Rich died, that idiot Freddie ended up in the trunk of a car. As far as I know, my uncle put him there. So I guess Uncle Rich wasn't all bad.

—AS TOLD TO MATTHEW FENTON
(Editor's Note: Names have been changed.)

What It Feels Like to Execute Someone

[By Donald Cabana, 58, former warden at Mississippi State Penitentiary at Parchman]

I killed four men in five years as warden and I recall them all so vividly, as if I was still standing next to the gas chamber. As warden every part of the execution was my responsibility, from picking out the members of my strap-down team, to contacting the victim's family, to ordering the inmate's last meal, to signaling the executioner to drop the cyanide. But no matter how tied up I always got in the details, I was never prepared when that gas chamber door slammed shut and the executioner said to me, "Warden, we're ready." Hearing "We're ready" was always like a cold splash of water in my face.

I knew that no one could move a muscle unless I gave the order. And the order never came out easily. Some wardens give a thumbs-up, but I always said something simple, like "Okay, let's do it." That's when the executioner flips the lever and the dish of cyanide crystals hits a pan of sulfuric acid under the chair. Ten seconds later, you start to see the gas rising. A few seconds later, it reaches his face. You'd probably think that the electric chair is more violent than the gas chamber, but the chamber is worse because it takes so damn long. Normally, the inmate will hold his breath, but it only makes it worse. They fight, so it's horrible. The eyes roll out of sight and you'll see a yellowish foam coming out of the mouth and nose. There are seizures. And they always claw at the arms of the chair with their fingers. It can take anywhere from thirty seconds to four and a half minutes for them to lose consciousness. Four and a half minutes is an eternity for a guy about to die. One guy, Connie Ray Evans, did exactly what I told him not to. I remember beating on the glass of the chamber screaming, "Jesus Christ, make him breathe."

In each of these executions, I watched these men die from my order and couldn't help wondering what my kids deep down thought about me. And then I still wonder what my God will ask of me when I meet Him. I guess I'll say that I did my job with compassion and a sense of dignity for everyone involved. That's the best you can do.

—AS TOLD TO GERSH KUNTZMAN

What It Feels Like
TO BE IN SOLITARY CONFINEMENT

[By Paul Wright, 38, McNeil Island Corrections Center, Prisoner #930783]

When I'm in solitary I think a lot about *One Day in the Life of Ivan Denisovich*. Alexander Solzhenitsyn says you "can never describe what it's like to be cold and to be hungry to someone who's never been cold and hungry." You can try to describe solitary, but there's only so much you can say.

It's a very tomblike existence. It's kind of like going into a submarine. The cells are bare concrete, a steel desk bolted to the wall, a steel toilet, and the only outside view is a strip window that's about 3 inches wide and 4 feet tall. It's continuously lit, 24 hours a day, and there are no clocks, so you get the timelessness effect. The guards won't tell you what time it is if you ask them.

More than anything, you get overwhelmed by the sleep deprivation because of the constant lighting. They give you a steel slab to sleep on with a plastic mattress. They give you sheets, but the plastic mattresses don't breathe, so you tend to get all sweaty and stick to them.

Sometimes you're locked up next to "the bangers." They're guys that bang on the metal furniture in the cell 24 hours a day. Years ago I was in a segregation unit in Walla Walla, and there was a guy named Martinez in the cell next to mine, and around 4 P.M. in the afternoon he would start banging his head against the toilet, and keep going until after midnight. That was the worst.

—AS TOLD TO DANIEL TORDAY

What It Feels Like to Swallow Swords

[By Brad Byers, 43, performer]

When I first started, it was the strangest sensation to have this cold steel blade in my esophagus, going down. Now it feels natural.

The epiglottis is the hardest part—that's the valve that seals off either the trachea or the esophagus. I'm able to move the epiglottis to open up the esophagus but not seal off the trachea, so I can breathe while I swallow the sword.

I can swallow up to ten swords. Each time a new sword is introduced into the esophagus, you have to control and suppress the gag reflex. The tighter it gets, the more difficult it is to control. If I do seven or more, sometimes my eyes water. When I do large numbers of swords, my esophagus is filled so much, and it's so close to the heart, I can actually feel my heart beating. I can see the swords move in time to my heart. With each thump-thump of my heart, the handles are doing a thump-thump. It's kind of like feeling your pulse.

I can give the swords a twist. It's an unnatural feeling. It feels most natural to lay the swords flat on the back of your throat like you would lay a tongue depressor. So when you rotate it, it's edgewise against your Adam's apple. That twisting thing gives my throat a real raw, dry feeling if I've overdone it. I scraped an actual hole in the back of my throat from too much performing.

I never get sick to my stomach. I can do an entire act after a heavy meal. In fact, I ate a heavy meal before that record attempt that was seen on the Guinness Book of World Records TV show. They set us at the studio, and I just ate everything I wanted.

I don't usually get nervous because then the esophagus will close up. But I got freaked out once. I was performing in Casper, Wyoming, at a shopping mall grand opening. At that time, I used to let people push the sword down my throat. I've always had women do it. But this time I chose a big, burly guy. He tried to act macho, but I noticed his hands were shaking a little bit. I knelt down on one knee and let him push it down. Then I gave him the stop signal, which I told him I would do, and I think to compensate for his feeling afraid, he pushed too far. The sword went down farther than I'd ever felt before. I felt a stretching sensation in the bottom of my stomach. It was like a balloon being stretched too deep by a pointed object. I had to pull his hand off it. I withdrew the sword and there was no blood so I thought I was okay and I finished the act with seven swords. When I pulled them out they were covered with blood.

Now I have people withdraw the blade from my mouth intead of pushing it down. You can't pull out a sword too far.

—AS TOLD TO MATT CLAUS

Part 8

What It Feels Like to Live and Die

What It Feels Like to Give Birth

[By Dee McManamy, 43, housewife]

▶ A contraction feels like the most painful gastric cramp you've ever had, or really bad indigestion. It happens almost where your intestines are, and it doubles you over. It's doing two things at the same time. One, your uterus is tightening. Two, at the bottom of the uterus is the cervix, the opening where the baby's gonna come out. The cervix opens from 0 to 10 centimeters, which is about 4 inches. It's actually drawing itself up and over the baby. It's like putting on a turtleneck sweater; you bunch up the neck at the top and make it bigger by stretching it. The whole thing pulls back over the head of the baby. And it really, really hurts. The pain comes in waves with the contractions, which get longer and more intense and closer together. As I was getting to labor and delivery the contractions were intense enough that I couldn't walk. I would have to stop, have the contraction, and then move on.

You feel a fullness when the baby starts coming out. Once the baby's head comes out, they stop you. Once you have started to push, that's all you want to do. Pushing feels really good. You're on your back, you have your legs drawn back, you have your thighs as close to your chest as possible, your legs spread full apart, your arms under your thighs almost like you're squatting but you're on your back, and the push-

The baby pictured is not McManamy's, although he is cute.

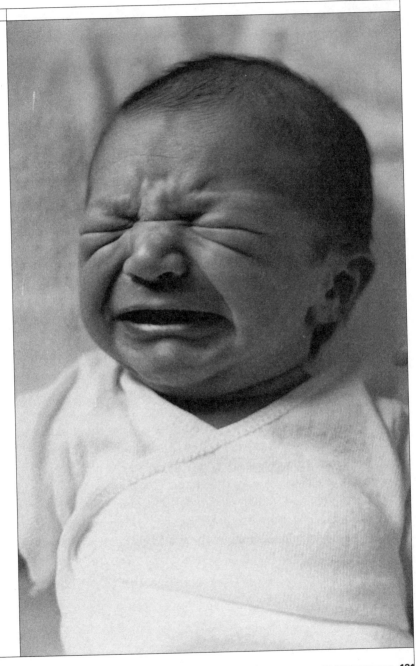

ing sensation is *exactly* the same as taking a poop. It's like you're having the biggest crap of your life.

You're doing this in front of total strangers. And when you're doing this, you're peeing, you're pooping for real—and it's somebody's job to clean that up.

The contractions at this point hurt so much, and you're so concentrated, that you actually fall sound asleep between contractions—even though they're only a couple of minutes apart, or less. Then my husband would wake me to tell me that it was coming, and I'd wake up and push, and then I was just dead asleep.

When the head is out, then you gotta get one shoulder, and then the whole baby just slides out. I've never run a marathon, but there's an incredible sense of relief and release. And there's this huge rush of blood and amniotic fluid and tissue, that just, *foom*, comes right out of you. It feels really good.

It's totally incomparable and indescribable. It's just a wall of warm liquid and gelatinous stuff. And then you still have to get the placenta out, and that takes another twenty or thirty minutes of pushing and contractions. There's just this rush of endorphins, and I never experienced anything like it. Suddenly there's no pain at all. And this incredible sense of accomplishment comes over you. You feel like you're in a parade, like a gladiator, like the victor. To be honest, it's a little like taking a hallucinatory drug—it's like you just took mushrooms. Colors are brighter, and everything just feels different, like you're looking at the world through new eyes.

—AS TOLD TO DANIEL TORDAY

What It Feels Like

TO WAKE FROM A COMA

[By Mike Carlo, 29, marketing manager]

A coma is like being in a deep sleep in which you can hear what's going on. This is how I know: I was eleven years old, riding a bicycle across an intersection in Lebanon, Ohio, when I got hit by a pickup truck going about 25 miles an hour. It was the first day of spring, 1986. I don't remember the collision, but I'm told I was thrown about 30 feet. I landed on my head and was knocked out of my shoes. The whole left side of my head was shattered. My sister says I was screaming and fighting with people who were trying to tend to me. The doctors gave me a 0 to 5 percent chance of surviving. They did surgery to remove parts of my fractured skull from my brain. After the first surgery, I went into a coma, which made the doctors feel a little better because my body had stabilized. A coma is a good thing. I'm not a doctor, so I don't know the medical terms, but when you're in a coma your body kind of goes on autopilot and does what it needs to in order to stay alive. There are different types of comas. I was in the deepest one, where your eyes are shut.

They had me hooked up with respirators and ventilators head to toe. Four days later I woke up. I can vaguely remember being very confused. I had no idea what had happened to me. The truth of the matter is, I felt fine. When they took the ventilator out, I asked: "How's Francis?" Turns out, Francis was the kid in the hospital bed next to mine. I'd never seen Francis in that four days because my eyes were shut. But I'd heard people talk about Francis. Francis had passed away the day before I'd woken up.

—AS TOLD TO
CAL FUSSMAN

What It Feels Like to Be in a Plane . . .

[By Ellen Hassman, 55, retired advertising executive]

It happened years ago, in the Caribbean on an airliner. But with great clarity and equal intensity, my memory is able to put me into that seat in the back of the plane just moments before the crash. Trays were in the upright position, and all handheld luggage was stored for landing. Being a nervous flyer to begin with, I remember feeling great relief when I heard the wheels touch the runway.

Then it happened. The plane began to increase in speed rather than decrease. I knew something was wrong. I can still feel the blood drain from my face. My hands became moist and began to shake. The plane shook and rattled, trying to lift into the air again. People began to talk louder, then they began to scream. The plane veered sharply to the left, and my body was thrown against the window. I looked at the ground as it reached up for us, and I knew we were going to crash.

My life didn't flash in front of my eyes. I saw no bright lights. I shook, I cried, and I cursed. A stream of curse words came forth from my mouth as if I were quoting a David Mamet play. I was angry. I didn't want to feel pain. I wanted to live, and I wanted to die quickly. I cried for my life that would never be. I didn't cry for those whom I would leave behind. Why should I? They would still be very much alive, and my envy fueled my anger. My tears were solely for me and the "why me" of it. I remember being angry at those who were screaming, because their screams were disturbing my precious last moments. And then I heard nothing but the sound of wrenching metal as the body of the plane met the ground, first class first.

I closed my eyes, and the screeching sound of metal twisting and tearing ripped through my head. I covered my ears with my hands, trying to stop the assault, and then we began to slide. We slid forever, like a car out of control on ice. I felt as if I were on one of those whip rides I used to go on as a child.

I opened my eyes to the sun shining on my face. There was nothing in front of me. The body of the plane had broken away at my feet. The stewardess and I were the only ones in the detached section of the plane's tail. In front of us, we could see the rest of the plane and the passengers continuing to slide as they headed toward disaster and eventual explosion. Now their screams filled me with sorrow. I jumped down to the ground unharmed. More than thirty people died.

Crash

What It Feels Like to Be 105 Years Old

[By Jenny Lundy, retired grocer]

You heard about me? That I'm an old lady? I was born in 1897 and I've seen a lot in the world. I've seen everything there is to see. You look back and tell yourself, "What have I been doing all these years?"

I'm in a wheelchair, sir. And I'm in a walker. Some days I feel good. According to the weather. If the weather's bad, then I have aches and pains. When the weather gets bad, your joints hurt all over. You get moody once in a while, and you start to think, "I don't believe I'm this age. What was I doing in my fifties, my forties, my thirties—what was I doing?"

The whole world is different, sir. The whole world is upside down. There were times when things were better. It's a long story, sir. They have it much easier today. What did they do before they had television? They played cards. We have nice bridge games over here in the village. It costs us fifty cents to get into the clubhouse. The real old people, believe me, they know how to play bridge—they can teach you a thing or two.

A day is short and the nights are long. Sometimes I lie in bed and I can't fall asleep. I think that God was good to me, that he gave me the health I have. I think what a wonderful life it is. I think about my mother. I had a sister and a brother, and they both passed away. I never knew my father.

One gentleman recently asked me if I wanted to have a cup of tea with him. I said, "No, thank you, I'm not that thirsty." And that's the way it is. What else can I tell you, sir? Wait, you get to be 105, and you'll find out.

People are very respectful. Very nice. They do look at me like I'm some kind of freak. They want to know the wonders of how I've lived this long. But is there some kind of secret? No. I know from the paper there's some people older than I. I'm as old as God gives me life. As long as God wants me on the world. When I'm ready, I'll have to take my bed. Okay?

—AS TOLD TO WILL GEORGANTAS

What It Feels Like
TO ATTEMPT SUICIDE

[By "Lee Garrett," 34, writer]

Sitting on the kitchen counter was a glass bottle of sleeping pills, mostly small and blue and diamond shaped, though some were white and oblong. I choked a handful down with a glass of orange juice. By the time I had to take the fourth handful, it got hard to swallow. When it was done, I had probably taken six handfuls. I didn't want to take more than that for fear of causing a gag reflex.

I went to lie down in bed. It was unmade from that morning and surprisingly cool for August. I lay flat on my back. For some reason, I crossed my arms over my chest, like I had been prepared for a coffin.

What do you think about as you wait to die? Do you think about the people who hurt you? Who "caused" this? The people you want to hurt? Yes, those things I did think about. And how everyone would be sorry. A couple of times I tried half-heartedly to pray, calling on God to forgive me. I bargained: If depression is an illness, as diagnosable as cancer, then God can't blame a suicide any more than God can blame a cancer victim for dying. Right? But suicides *do* have a more active hand in their deaths than the critically ill. . . .

I don't know how long I lay there before the phone rang—maybe fifteen or twenty minutes. The machine picked up. The voice identified itself as Officer So-and-So. "I'm calling to check on you. We received a call that earlier this morning you threatened suicide. If you don't talk to me now, we will send officers to your apartment." Wanting to head off a police raid, I got out of bed and walked, wobbly and dizzy, to the phone. And then I lied.

Back in bed, dying, my thoughts were random. Song lyrics played in my head (which I thought was good since it would eat up time and keep me from changing my mind). It was an odd hit parade: Leonard Cohen's "Suzanne" and the final refrain of Annie Lennox's "Why." I thought of the firing, the episode in my office earlier that day and how degrading it was and how it had felt like a dream. I thought about the TV I had watched the night before, the book I was reading but wouldn't ever finish. I reminded myself that I would soon know what death would be like.

Occasionally, my thoughts grew optimistic and I thought of jobs I could apply for, places I could move, favors I could call in. But it was easier just to lie there. And each time I made that decision—to just lie there and die—I felt relief. I wouldn't have to deal with the embarrassment of filing for unemployment or facing my family. . . .

But my body fought. My heart began to beat surprisingly hard—aren't sleeping pills supposed to slow it down? I panicked: What if the pills don't kill me?

I tried to fall asleep. My body began to twitch. The dying was painful. What happened to softly floating toward the light? I imagined my heart hitting against my rib cage.

My eyes sprang open. Then the room around me appeared, oddly, more . . . clear. I wondered if I was dead.

At some point—I can't tell how many minutes had passed, maybe twenty, maybe thirty—I decided not to die. That didn't mean I wanted to live. It was just that I didn't want to die. There's a difference.

So I called 911.

In the ER, I was hooked up to an IV, a blood pressure gauge, and an EKG. I was given a cup of charcoal and water that looked like tar. It would make me vomit the dissolving pills in my stomach. I drank it and promptly fell into a drug-induced sleep. I woke up occasionally, only long enough to puke into a plastic tub that they gave me.

(Editor's Note: Name has been changed.)

What It Feels Like to Have a Parachute Fail

[By Ray Maynard, 56, owner of Skydive Long Island, commercial pilot]

▶ I've jumped almost three thousand times. In all those jumps, I'd say I had serious problems maybe a dozen times. That comes to what percentage? Less than half of 1 percent? Those aren't bad odds. That has to be close to your chances of getting hit by lightning.

The most serious trouble I ever had was during a demonstration jump. People who are throwing parties will sometimes hire you to jump into the event to kick things off. From a professional sky diver's point of view, these are very basic jumps. Almost boring.

So I'm hired to do a demonstration jump at the Hunter Mountain Ski Resort in upstate New York. Just step out of the airplane and pull the cord. Let everyone on the ground "ooh" and "ah" about the pretty colors on the chute. Hop and pop. You're done in less than a half hour and it's easy work. Helps pay the bills.

Anyway, I jump and pull, and I'm jerked to one side. Right away, I know something is seriously screwed up. I look into the chute and it's partially deployed: fully inflated on one side and not inflated at all on the other side, because lines from the rigging have tangled over the top of the chute.

This is a major problem. It's actually a lot more dangerous than a chute that doesn't open at all. When it doesn't open at all, you just get rid of it and go to your reserve. But here, once I was jerked to the right, I'm being whipped in a circle, like

I'm in a washing machine going at full speed. In less than a second, I've been lifted almost horizontal, parallel to the ground, and I'm moving in a circle at more than 100 miles per hour. The center of the circle is the chute, just above my head. My legs and feet are at the edge of the circle. And the horizontal spin I'm caught in is nearly as fast as a helicopter blade. It's like riding a boomerang through a wind tunnel.

I know I'm in trouble and I have to get rid of the bad parachute. But the g-forces that work on your body in a spin like that do two things. One, they make it incredibly difficult to raise your arms to the center of your chest, where the emergency cord is. Second, because all the force is pulling away from the center of the spin, all of the blood in your body is rushing away from your head, toward your lower extremities. I can feel myself getting light-headed and I know I'm going to pass out in a few more seconds. So I'm trying to reach for the emergency cord that will jettison the main chute and deploy the backup. But it's like trying to lift 100-pound barbells when you're half asleep. I know if I don't get to the cord and pull it, I'm going to die. Finally, my arms reach up and my fingertips grasp the cord. I yank, the main chute blows away, and the secondary opens.

I'm safe, although the blood leaving my head feels like I have the worst hangover that any human being has ever experienced. This was all in less than seven, eight seconds.

I touch down close to my target, less than half a mile away. Which isn't bad, considering what I've just been through. Anyway, all the drunk ski bums watching from the deck of the bar are cheering like crazy. I think they're glad that I'm safe, and then it hits me. They never knew I was in trouble. They thought the spinout and the second chute were all part of the show.

—AS TOLD TO MATTHEW FENTON

What It Feels Like to Die

[By Cassandra Musgrave, 53, spiritual consultant]

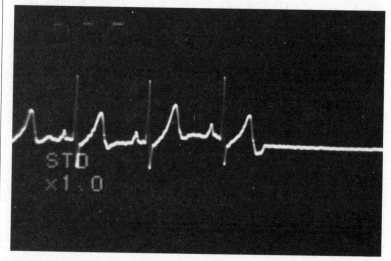

I was waterskiing and I fell, and the rope twisted around my left arm, dragging me under. It was like falling under an incredible waterfall where you could not possibly stand up. It's funny the thoughts that come—I actually thought, "If I die, my mother's going to be so mad at me...."

Soon, I felt my spirit floating out of my body and saw my body being dragged behind the boat—I was above my body, looking down. I didn't feel concerned. Then my spirit was moving through a dark tunnel about 5 or 6 feet wide. It didn't seem scary, but I was alone and felt like I was being pulled very rapidly toward another dimension.

Coming out of the tunnel, there were incredible colors and flowers like we don't see on Earth. They were different hues and different colors that are impossible to describe because they don't exist here. And then I found myself in another place and it felt very beautiful and very normal, like I'd been there before. I was out in the heavens. I saw stars and galaxies and it felt like I was on something solid but I never really looked down so I was probably just floating around out there. It felt like I was me, but me without a physical body. I wasn't concerned that I didn't have a body—I was enraptured by this wonderful place.

Then this being appeared to me—it was Melchizedek, a high priest from the Bible. I wasn't raised with any conscious awareness of him, but I recognized him—like if you saw your long-lost grandmother, you'd know her. It was warm, wonderful, and comforting there, and he was tall and beautiful with robes and velvet and things. And he asked, "Are you ready to come?" Then he showed me things that would help me to make that decision. I saw my young son onshore. I saw that I would be drowned and they would pull me up on the boat and I would lose the bottom of my bathing suit. I was thinking, "Cover me up!" and "I shopped a long time for that bathing suit." I mean, you're still you.

So I saw that they would take me to shore and it would take a long time for the ambulance to come and that they would put me on the ground and try and resuscitate me but I'd be dead. And Denny, my boyfriend, would never get over it.

Given those things and so much more—and there WAS a lot more to the story that I can't fit into a short piece like this one—I decided to come back. All of a sudden I was in the water just like I'd seen, except I wasn't dead. So I'm coughing up water, and my friend dives in and drags me up on the boat and the rope is all messed up in my arm, just like I'd seen, and I'd lost the bottom of my bathing suit, just like I'd seen.

—AS TOLD TO ELIZABETH EINSTEIN

ABOUT THE AUTHOR

A. J. JACOBS is a senior editor at *Esquire* magazine. He is also the author of *The Two Kings: Jesus and Elvis* and *America Off-Line*. He lives in New York.